■ The Vermont State Constitution

The Oxford Commentaries on the State Constitutions of the United States
G. Alan Tarr, Series Editor

Professor G. Alan Tarr, Director of the Center on State Constitutional Studies at Rutgers University, serves as General Editor for this important new series which in its entirety will cover each of the 50 states. Each volume of The Oxford Commentaries on the State Constitutions of the United States contains a historical overview of the state's constitutional development, plus a section-by-section analysis of the state's current constitution. Other features included in the volumes are the text of the state's constitution, a bibliographic essay, table of cases, and index. This series provides essential reference tools for those investigating state constitutional development and constitutional law.

The Vermont State Constitution

William C. Hill

Foreword by Thomas P. Salmon

THE OXFORD COMMENTARIES ON THE STATE CONSTITUTIONS OF THE UNITED STATES
G. Alan Tarr, Series Editor

OXFORD
UNIVERSITY PRESS

OXFORD
UNIVERSITY PRESS

Oxford University Press, Inc., publishes works that further Oxford University's objective of excellence in research, scholarship, and education.

Oxford New York
Auckland Cape Town Dar es Salaam Hong Kong Karachi Kuala Lumpur Madrid Melbourne Mexico City Nairobi New Delhi Shanghai Taipei Toronto

With offices in
Argentina Austria Brazil Chile Czech Republic France Greece Guatemala Hungary Italy Japan Poland Portugal Singapore South Korea Switzerland Thailand Turkey Ukraine Vietnam

Previously published in 1992 by Greenwood Press

Published by Oxford University Press, Inc.
198 Madison Avenue, New York, New York 10016

Oxford is a registered trademark of Oxford University Press
Oxford University Press is a registered trademark of Oxford University Press, Inc.

Library of Congress Cataloging-in-Publication Data

Hill, William C.
The Vermont state constitution / William C. Hill ; foreword by Thomas P. Salmon.
p. cm. — (The Oxford commentaries on the state constitutions of the United States)
Includes bibliographical references and index.
ISBN 978-0-19-977902-4 (hardback)
1. Constitutions—Vermont. I. Title.
KFV4011973.A6 H545 2011
342.74302'3—dc22 2011001555

Note to Readers
This publication is designed to provide accurate and authoritative information in regard to the subject matter covered. It is based upon sources believed to be accurate and reliable and is intended to be current as of the time it was written. It is sold with the understanding that the publisher is not engaged in rendering legal, accounting, or other professional services. If legal advice or other expert assistance is required, the services of a competent professional person should be sought. Also, to confirm that the information has not been affected or changed by recent developments, traditional legal research techniques should be used, including checking primary sources where appropriate.

(Based on the Declaration of Principles jointly adopted by a Committee of the American Bar Association and a Committee of Publishers and Associations.)

CONTENTS

■ SERIES FOREWORD

In 1776, following the declaration of independence from England, the former colonies began to draft their own constitutions. Their handiwork attracted widespread interest, and draft constitutions circulated up and down the Atlantic seaboard, as constitution-makers sought to benefit from the insights of their counterparts in sister states. In Europe, the new constitutions found a ready audience seeking enlightenment from the American experiments in selfgovernment. Even the delegates to the Constitutional Convention of 1787, despite their reservations about the course of political events in the states during the decade after independence, found much that was useful in the newly adopted constitutions. And when James Madison, fulfilling a pledge given during the campaign for the ratification of the Constitution, drafted the Federal Bill of Rights, he found his model in the famous Declaration of Rights of the Virginia Constitution.

By the 1900s, however, few people would have looked to state constitutions for enlightenment. Instead, a familiar litany of complaints was heard whenever state constitutions were mentioned. State constitutions were too long and too detailed, combining basic principles with policy prescriptions and prohibitions that had no place in the fundamental law of a state. By including such provisions, it was argued, state constitutions deprived state governments of the flexibility they needed to respond effectively in changing circumstances. This—among other factors—encouraged political reformers to look to the federal government, which was not plagued by such constitutional constraints, thereby shifting the locus of political initiative away from the states. Meanwhile, civil libertarians concluded that state bills of rights, at least as interpreted by state courts, did not adequately protect rights and therefore looked to the federal courts and the federal Bill of Rights for redress. As power and responsibility shifted from the states to Washington, so too did the attention of scholars, the legal community, and the general public.

During the early 1970s, however, state constitutions were "rediscovered." The immediate impetus for this rediscovery was former President Richard Nixon's appointment of Warren Burger to succeed Earl Warren as Chief Justice of the United States Supreme Court. To civil libertarians, this appointment seemed to signal a decisive shift in the Supreme Court's jurisprudence, because Burger was expected to lead the Court away from the liberal activism that had characterized the Warren Court. They therefore sought ways to safeguard the gains they had achieved for defendants, racial minorities, and the poor during Warren's tenure from erosion by the Burger Court. In particular, they began to look to state bills of rights to secure the rights of defendants and to support the other civil liberties claims that they advanced in state courts.

This "new judicial federalism," as it came to be called, quite quickly advanced beyond its initial concern to evade the mandates of the Burger Court. Indeed, less than two decades after it originated, it has become a national phenomenon. When judges and scholars turned their attention to state constitutions, they discovered an unsuspected richness. They found not only provisions that paralleled the Federal Bill of Rights but also constitutional guarantees of the right to privacy and of gender equality, for example, that had no analogue in the U.S. Constitution. Careful examination of the text and history of state guarantees revealed important differences between even those provisions that most resembled federal guarantees and their federal counterparts. Looking beyond state declarations of rights, scholars and jurists discovered affirmative constitutional mandates to state governments to address such important policy concerns as education and housing. Taken altogether, these discoveries underlined the importance for the legal community of developing a better understanding of state constitutions.

William C. Hill's excellent study of the Vermont Constitution is the latest contribution to the series, the Oxford Commentaries on the State Constitutions of the United States, which reflects the renewed interest in state constitutions and will contribute to our knowledge about them. Because the constitutional tradition of each state is distinctive, the volume begins with the history and development of constitutionalism in Vermont. It then provides the complete text of the state's current constitution, with each section accompanied with commentary that explains the provision and traces its origins and its interpretation by the courts and by other governmental bodies. Finally, the book concludes with a bibliography, a table of cases cited in the volume, and a topical index.

G. Alan Tarr

■ FOREWORD

In this scholarly book former Supreme Court Justice William C. Hill makes a singular contribution to our understanding of the Vermont Constitution as a forceful presence in the Vermont justice system. The historical underpinnings of this work focus the reader on the first stirrings of the Independent Republic of Vermont and the Convention at Windsor where our forefathers dared to prescribe a bold and imaginative Constitution including Universal Manhood, Suffrage, and the Prohibition of Slavery. Then followed a turbulent fourteen years wherein the basic plan and framework of the Constitution served to guide our early governance, while what was to become the fourteenth state of the Union was buffeted by adversaries from the North, the East, and the West. By 1793, two years after admission, the basic Constitution, as we now know it, was fundamentally in place.

Although the Federal Constitution has a similar origin and purpose, the two documents are not the same. There are imposing differences both in history and in text which are definitively explored. The Vermont Constitution has emerged as a source of greater protection of the rights of citizens of this State than its federal counterpart. The author and his esteemed colleague, the late Justice Thomas L. Hayes, are largely responsible for this development.

In sum, our State Constitution has emerged as a meaningful vehicle for the advancement of justice in Vermont. It has proven capable of providing a final appellate answer to a claim or a grievance where appropriate invocation of its protections is artfully sought. This book coincides with a resurgence of Federalism in this country in which Appellate Courts continue to find that individual rights guaranteed by State Constitutions are broader than those secured by their federal counterpart. This scholarly and comprehensive exploration of Vermont's Constitution will long endure as an invaluable historic resource.

Thomas P. Salmon
President, the University of Vermont;
former Governor of Vermont

■ ACKNOWLEDGMENTS

I am indebted to D. Gregory Sanford, state archivist, and his staff for assistance in exploring sources of the Vermont Constitution contained in the archives of the state, and equally grateful to Paul S. Gillies, Deputy Secretary of State, for enlightening discussions on the content of the documents. Additional sources were available at the Bailey-Howe Library of the University of Vermont. I am especially grateful to J. Kevin Graffagnino, Wilbur Curator, Connell B. Gallagher, Assistant Director for Special Collections, and the staff, each of whom responded readily to my frequent requests for necessary sources. I was fortunate to have the expert secretarial assistance of Brenda Hughes of Monkton, Vermont. The critical reviews of several drafts by Professor G. Alan Tarr of Rutgers University were illuminating, and his patience was a constant source of encouragement to me.

I wish to express my appreciation to my daughter, Toni Hill, for her technical assistance and her help in organizing the text.

I am most grateful for the valuable suggestions and the unfailing support of Grace, my wife, without whose patient reading of numerous drafts this volume would not have been completed.

PART ONE

The History of the Vermont Constitution

Vermont is one of the smallest of the fifty states in territory and population. It is bounded on the north by the province of Quebec in Canada, containing Montreal and Quebec, cities that loomed large in Vermont's history; its eastern border is the west bank of the Connecticut River; its southern boundary is an arbitrary line separating Vermont from Massachusetts and New York; and on the west, it is protected by the waters of Lake Champlain, scence of decisive battles in the American Revolution and the War of 1812.

The French explorer Samuel de Champlain recorded in his journal the earliest European view of the territory now known as Vermont on July 4, 1609, as his flotilla made its way down the lake that bears his name. More than fifty years passed before the French made an effort to settle in the territory; then in 1666 in the northwest, on an island in Lake Champlain still called Isle La Motte, they built Fort St. Anne. It was not until 1724, however, that the English of the Massachusetts Bay Colony built and garrisoned Fort Dummer in southeastern Vermont, on the west bank of the Connecticut River, in what is now the town of Dummerston.

In 1741 the governor of the New Hampshire colony, Benning Wentworth, determined from the colony charter that the territory west of the Connecticut River was part of his domain, and that it was within his power as governor to sell of areas to any persons or groups willing to pay for the title. The land was almost entirely untouched forest which made fine farms when cleared. Wentworth laid out towns generally six miles square and sold them to groups from Connecticut and Massachusetts; some were land speculators, others were interested in settling. This new territory became known as the Hampshire Grants.

Although the English had garrisoned Fort Dummer, Vermont historians have established that the first English settlement on the western bank of the Connecticut River in the Hampshire Grants was located at Westminster. In 1741, however, the title to this territory was not as clear as Benning Wentworth wished. Fearing that the New York Colony might have an interest in the lands lying between the Connecticut River and Lake Champlain, Wentworth initiated a correspondence with the governor of New York to clarify the boundaries. This correspondence served only to generate an ownership dispute between their two colonies so heated that the matter was finally referred to the British government, and it was not until 1764 that a British order-in-council declared the west bank of the Connecticut River to be the boundary between the two colonies. Wentworth, however, had not been idle: from 1741 until the determination of the boundary in 1764, he had sold at least 128 townships in the disputed territory to various groups throughout New England.

The first act of the New York speculators to lead to conflict between New York and the settlers of the Hampshire Grants occurred when, instead of accepting a small rent from the settlers who had already purchased land, the speculators demanded not only rent but a new purchase fee. This prompted the settlers to commission Capt. Samuel Robinson of Bennington to take a petition to the king asking relief from New York's action, and in 1767 George III issued a further order-in-council forbidding New York to regrant the Hampshire Grants already settled. New York paid no attention to the order, and its governor continued to sell parcels of the Vermont territory.

There is no evidence that the settlers in the Hampshire Grants cared whether New York or New Hampshire exercised jurisdiction over them; in fact, they accepted the courts and the officials appointed by New York for all legal purposes except the foreclosing of farms for failure to pay a second fee, which would have resulted in eviction. They simply refused to be evicted from their lands for the fee or the quitrents also required.

In 1769, the New Yorkers, determined to pursue their claims, sent surveyors to the Grants to survey the farm of James Breakenridge located west of the Green Mountains, but they were driven off by Breakenridge and his neighbors. A further attempt again met with resistance, this time by the Green Mountain Boys, a group of local patriots who had been organized under the leadership of Ethan Allen to protect the settlers against any Yorker action.

Any consideration of Vermont's constitutional history must include the Green Mountains, the range dividing Vermont internally from the north to the south; the stand taken in the Hampshire Grants against New York was all the more remarkable because this ever-present barrier between the eastern and western grants made communications among the various towns so difficult.

The anti-New Yorker feeling, furthermore, was not unanimous. Some of the towns in the southeastern area wanted to join New York and pay the extra fees, while other settlers opposed any form of colony control and advocated a separate district. Internal conflicts continued among the settlers favoring allegiance to New York, New Hampshire, or Massachusetts, or favoring independence, until Vermont's admission into the United States as the fourteenth state in 1791.

Vermont literature abounds with references to threats of mayhem or worse made by opposing settlers, particularly the Green Mountain Boys and the New Yorkers, but except for two recorded fatalities in the so-called Westminster Massacre in March 1775, no person was seriously injured in the Grants prior to the outbreak of the Revolutionary War.

The Westminster Massacre was a small incident in itself. Settlers in the area around Westminster, in the east, had attempted to seize control of the Cumberland County courthouse, where cases were being heard by New York-appointed authorities, to prevent the March 1775 term of that court from being held. A contingent of Green Mountain Boys from the west arrived and came to the aid of the settlers. We cannot dismiss the event, however, without noting that this was the first known occasion on which the two sides of the mountain came together in any political context.

Another step toward unity occurred in Westminster the following month, when a convention of eastside towns met to voice their grievances against the government of New York and requested that a remonstrance against the "unjustifiable conduct" of New York be prepared by a committee to consist of two eastsiders and Col. Ethan Allen of the westside. It was the first conscious effort of the east to include the west in its proceedings; but before the commission to prepare the remonstrance reached Colonel Allen, the battle of Lexington and Concord occurred and the American Revolution had begun.

More conventions were held, on both sides of the mountain. On January 16, 1776, at a convention in Dorset on the west side, Heman Allen, another of the ubiquitous Allen clan, was authorized to present a petition to Congress asking for inclusion in that august body and pledging loyalty to Congress but not to New York. He reported to a second Dorset convention on July 24, 1776, which again proclaimed its loyalty to Congress and its continued hostility to New York, and it also declared the Grants a "separate district."

At a third convention in Dorset, on September 25, 1776, representatives from forty-four towns were present, of which eleven were from the Connecticut valley. This time, meeting and taking joint actions, the east and west together reiterated grievances against New York and appointed committees, including a committee to petition Congress for admission into its ranks.

ADOPTION OF THE CONSTITUTION

The conventions then began to meet in the east, and on January 15, 1777, a small convention, representing only seven westside and eleven eastside towns, met in Westminster and declared its independence from Great Britain in the following language:

> That the district of territory comprehending and usually known by the name and description of the New Hampshire Grants, of right ought to be, and is hereby declared forever hereafter, to be considered as a separate, free and independent jurisdiction or state; by the name, and forever hereafter to be called, known and distinguished by the name of New Connecticut.[1]

The new state then appointed a committee to carry a petition to Congress again requesting admission to the Union. Before the petition could be acted upon by Congress, the committee returned, bearing a letter from Dr. Thomas Young of Philadelphia, a boyhood friend of Ethan Allen who had become interested in the affairs of the new state. His letter read, in part:

> I have taken the minds of several leading members in the honourable Continental Congress, and can assure you, that you have nothing to do but to send attested copies of the recommendation to take up Government to every township in your district, and invite all your freeholders and inhabitants to meet in their respective townships, and choose members for a General Convention, to meet at an early date, to choose delegates for the General Congress, a Committee of Safety, and to form a Constitution for your State. Your friends here tell me, that some are in doubt, whether delegates from your district should be admitted into Congress; I tell you to organize fairly, and make the experiment, and I will insure you success, at the risk of my reputation as a man of honour or common sense; indeed, they can by no means refuse you; you have as good a right to choose how you will be governed, and by whom, as they had.[2]

Following the Declaration of Independence each of the thirteen colonies was ordered to prepare a state constitution. For use as a model, Dr. Young had forwarded the Constitution of Pennsylvania.

New York had adopted a constitution early in 1777 that did nothing to quiet the fears of many Vermonters. It contained provisions indicating that the new fees and quitrents would be continued. These two incidents triggered the constitutional convention that formed the Vermont Constitution of 1777.

---

[1] E. P. Walton, *Records of the Council of Safety and Governor and Council of the State of Vermont vol. 1* (Montpelier Steam Press of J & J. M. Poland, 1873), 41.

[2] Ira Allen, *The Natural and Political History of the State of Vermont* (1798; reprint. London: Charles E. Tuttle, 1969), 59.

Another convention met with Young's documents in hand at Windsor on the east side on June 4, 1777. Before Congress had a chance to again deny admission, the convention changed the name of the district from New Connecticut to Vermont, appointed a committee to draft a constitution for consideration, and adjourned until July 2.

When they reconvened, General John Burgoyne was travelling along the shores of Lake Champlain with a large army composed of Hessian mercenaries and Indians as well as regular British troops. The only existing record of the Windsor Convention of July 2, 1777, is found in Ira Allen's history of Vermont:

> Soon after the return of the Commissioners from Congress, Ira Allen printed and published a pamphlet, shewing the right the people had to form a Government, which, with Dr. Young's Letter, were spread through the State, and measures taken to convene a Convention, which met at Windsor in June 1777, to form a constitution, and appointed a committee to make a draft of a constitution, and passed a resolution, recommending it to each town to elect and send Representatives to a Convention, to meet at Windsor in July following. William Marsh, James Mead, Ira Allen, and Captain Salisbury, were appointed a Committee to wait on the Commander of Ticondaroga [*sic*] Fort, and consult with him respecting the regulations and defence of the frontiers, then adjourned to the 4th [the adjournment to, and the meeting at Windsor were July 2, instead of the 4th] of July, 1777, to meet at the same place. While the Committee was at Ticondaroga [*sic*], General Burgoyne, with his army, appeared on the lake, and resting at Crown Point, he sent a scout of about 300, mostly Indians, to land at the mouth of Otter Creek, to annoy the frontiers of the State. General Poor refused to allow any troops to the Committee for the defence of the frontiers, but allowed Colonel Warner to go with the Committee, who soon raised men sufficient to repel the assailants. All who were members of the Convention left the militia, and repaired to Windsor on July 4th, 1777. A draft of a constitution was laid before the Convention, and read. The business being new, and of great consequence, required serious deliberation. The Convention had it under consideration when the news of the evacuation of Ticondaroga [*sic*] arrived, which alarmed them very much, as thereby the frontiers of the State were exposed to the inroads of an enemy. The family of the President of the Convention, as well as those of many other members, were exposed to the foe. In this awful crisis the Convention was for leaving Windsor, but a severe thunderstorm came on, and gave them time to reflect, while other members, less alarmed at the news, called the attention of the whole to finish the Constitution, which was then reading paragraph by paragraph for the last time. This was done, and the Convention then appointed a Council of Safety to act during the recess, and the Convention adjourned.[3]

[3] Ibid., 62–63.

William Slade reported as follows:

> Previous to the adjournment, it was ordered that the first election, under the constitution, should be holden in December, 1777; and that the general assembly, thus elected, should meet at Bennington, in January, 1778. The publick attention, however, being arrested by the evacuation of Tyconderoga, and the progress of the enemy under General Burgoyne; the constitution was not printed, seasonably, to have the election holden in December. The convention was, therefore, summoned, by the Council of safety, to meet, at Windsor, on the 24th of December, 1777.
>
> They met; revised the constitution, and postponed the day of election until the first Tuesday of March, 1778, and the sitting of the Assembly until the second Thursday of the same month.[4]

Following the adoption of the constitution at Windsor a meeting of the Council of Safety was held in February 1778; it addressed the inhabitants of Vermont as follows:

> To the Inhabitants of the State of Vermont
>
> Gentlemen,
>
> The united and joint representatives of this state, in their general convention, held at Windsor, on the 2nd day of July last, did compose, and agree, unanimously, on a constitution for the future government and mutual advantage of its inhabitants. It was then proposed by the joint agreement of the said representatives, that such constitution should be printed, so as to have had them circulated among the inhabitants, seasonably, to have had the general election of representatives to compose the general assembly, in December last; who, by agreement, was to have met at Bennington, within this state, in the month of January last. But finding, by repeated experience, that the troubles of the war, and encroachments of the enemy would, of necessity, render it impossible, this council did think fit to again call on the members of the general convention, to meet; who, accordingly, met at Windsor, on the 24th day of December last, and did, unanimously, agree to postpone the day of election until the first Tuesday of March next, and the sitting of the assembly to be at Windsor, on the second Thursday of March next. The constitution is now printed, and will be distributed among the inhabitants of the several towns in this state, so early, that they may be perused before the day of election.[5]

Although based on the Pennsylvania Constitution of 1776, the constitution adopted in Vermont contained significant differences. For example, its preamble,

[4] William Slade, *Vermont State Papers* (Middlebury: J. W. Copeland, Printer, 1823), 80.
[5] Ibid., 81.

while including grievances against King George, was nevertheless largely devoted to listing complaints against New York (see Appendix 1).

Of greater significance, it contained in its first section the first written constitutional prohibition against slavery of any of the early state constitutions, reading, in part:

> therefore no male person, born in this country, or brought from over sea, ought to be holden by law, to serve any person, as a servant, slave or apprentice, after he arrives at the age of twenty-one years, nor female in like manner, after she arrives at the age of eighteen years, unless they are bound by their own consent, after they arrive at such age or bound by law, for the payment of debts, damages, fines, costs or the like.

The distinction between male and female should be noted.

The 1777 Constitution also added a section permitting the taking of property by eminent domain: the ability of the government to take property without the consent of the governed, which opened the way for development of the public utilities and transportation so vitally important for economic growth. Furthermore, the section of eminent domain, as written then, was stated in terms that essentially remain in the present constitution. Another section was added denying a plaintiff a writ of attachment of a debtor's estate or person without an oath or affirmation that there was danger of the property being dissipated before judgment. Finally, the last new section in the Declaration of Rights prohibited transportation out of the state for the trial of any offense committed within the state. It did,in contrast to the Pennsylvania Constitution, grant universal suffrage to all men over the age of twenty-one.

It was in the second chapter that the plan or frame of government was announced. Vermont substantially followed the plan of government set out in the Pennsylvania Constitution: both constitutions provided for government by a unicameral House of Representatives and a governor and Governor's Council as executive; both established courts of justice, and both made provision for a Council of Censors (the only constitutions in the United States with such a provision). The Council of Censors was to meet every seven years. Its function was expressed in the following language in Section 44:

> The said Council of Censors will also have power to call a Convention, to meet within two years after their sitting, if there appears to them an absolute necessity of amending any article of this constitution which may be defective—explaining such as may be thought not clearly expressed, and of adding such as are necessary for the preservation of the rights and happiness of the people; but the articles to be amended, and the amendments proposed, and such articles as are proposed to be added or abolished, shall be promulgated at least six months before the election of such convention, for the previous consideration of the people, that they may have an opportunity of instructing their delegates on the subject.

The Council of Censors was the only body authorized to propose amendments to the constitution.

The Constitution of 1777 was never adopted by the people of Vermont, nor did it hold any provision setting forth a method whereby it would be adopted. The Windsor Convention constituted the only body that formally approved the Constitution of 1777. The state of Vermont was organized, officials elected, and the legislature convened all in accordance with the provisions of this convention without the approval of the people. Whether that approval would have been given is uncertain. We know that there was continued opposition to the formation of the state; we cannot, however, be sure of the strength of that opposition. Possibly the west side would have been overwhelmingly in favor of statehood while on the east side supporters would have encountered significant resistance from dissenters. According to Dorothy Canfield Fisher, one look at the New York constitution of 1777 sent the Vermont east siders to stand beside those west of the green mountains. General Jacob Bayley, leader of the Connecticut valley moderates, wrote to the New York Committee of Safety, "The people, before they saw the constitution, was not willing to trouble themselves about a separation from the state of New York, but now, almost to a man they are violent for it."[6]

Although the convention fully complied with Dr. Young's suggestion to adopt a constitution, the Continental Congress of the United States refused to admit the new fourteenth state until 1791, and Vermont remained until then a truly free and independent nation. It was, however, not free from the turmoil engendered by the grasping hands of its neighboring states. Nor was it free from internal bickering. It continued to exist because of the shrewdness and stubbornness of a group of fiercely independent leaders.

It was a characteristic effort that, during the balance of the Revolutionary War, these men were willing to go so far as to enter into negotiations with British leaders in Canada for eventual reinclusion of Vermont in the British Empire, which, among other factors, forced the Continental Congress to delay action on the request of New York that it be declared the owner of this upstart fledgling.

Yet, Vermont's independent existence led to requests by towns in New Hampshire on the east side of the Connecticut River to join it, and for a short time Vermont contained towns that had seceded from New Hampshire. Eventually, against their wishes, these towns were returned to their mother state. This not only served to avoid an armed conflict with New Hampshire, but also gained Vermont time to become better organized and more powerful. Even some New York towns petitioned to join. By playing state against state and negotiating with the British in Canada, Vermont was able to struggle through the revolutionary period independently.

---

[6] Dorothy Canfield Fisher. *Vermont Tradition* (Boston: Little, Brown, 1953), 119.

Vermont nevertheless remained faithful to the United States during this period. While it negotiated with Canada, it still had soldiers in the field helping General Washington. Men from the Green Mountains fought in the battles of Hubbardton and Bennington and were in the front ranks at Saratoga. Vermont remained the buffer against British incursions from Canada, through negotiations with Canada spread out over a long enough period effectively to deter another British advance into the United States from the north.

Amid all these machinations, the Continental Congress refused to act on petitions from New York and Vermont, and the government of Vermont continued to function under Chapter 2 (the plan or frame of Government) of the Constitution of 1777. No changes were permitted in that constitution, as we have noted, for seven years, and then only on recommendation of a Council of Censors. By the first septenary, after reviewing the events and the operation of the government, the first Council of Censors determined that the time for revision had come.

Vermont was fortunate to have in its first Council of Censors some of the outstanding men of the state. Although still under a threat from New York, they met during a time of peace, in 1785, and having determined that the constitution needed revision, in accordance with the constitutional directive, they called for a convention to be held in 1786 to consider their recommendations of amendment. In their address to this required convention they had reason to state the following:

> We can only in general observe, that, under God, this commonwealth is much indebted, even of its present existence as a separate community, to that undaunted firmness, and prudent vigilance for the public safety, which has usually maintained in the legislative and executive departments, since the era of our independence. At open war with the most potent nation in Europe;—frequently threatened with invasions from a sister State, and, by her insidious arts, a powerful disaffection, fomented within the bowels of this commonwealth—denied relief from the authority who alone, under Heaven, could give it;—we have reason to look up, with gratitude, to that Being who is wisdom, and by whom a few husbandmen, unexperienced in the art of governing, have been enabled to pilot the ship through storms and quicksands, into the haven of independence and safety; and to admire when we consider how much was to be done, and by whom, that it has been so well done.[7]

As the council reported, it wanted to make government wiser, more energetic, and less expensive. It also deemed "electing persons to judicial and executive trusts, during good behavior," dangerous in its vagueness, and wished to "guard against the future introduction of an aristocratic power, destructive

[7] Gillies and Sanford. *Records of the Council of Censors.* (Essex, Vt: Offset House, 1991), 59.

of the common weal, by providing that the same person should not, at one time, be invested with too many important offices."[8]

The convention called by the council met in June 1786 to consider the recommended changes to the Constitution of 1777. In making their proposals of change to the convention, the council redrafted the constitution and incorporated the proposed changes into the original text. Upon adoption by the convention, this became the Constitution of 1786.

The convention did not, however, adopt the constitution exactly as the council had presented it; four new articles and three new sections were adopted at its recommendation. It also adopted numerous amendments to specific articles and sections of the Constitution of 1777 (Chapter 1 provisions were denoted articles, while Chapter 2 provisions were denoted sections).

A new Article 4 guaranteed a right to a remedy in the following language:

> Every person within this commonwealth ought to find a certain remedy, by having recourse to the laws, for all injuries or wrongs which he may receive in his person, property or character; he ought to obtain right and justice freely, and without being obliged to purchase it; completely and without any denial; promptly and without delay; conformably to the laws.

This article was probably suggested because the council had censured the legislature for actions taken by that branch that usurped the functions of the courts.

Article 16 (now Article 14) was new to the 1786 Constitution. It provided that freedom of speech and debate in the legislature was so essential that "it cannot be the foundation of any accusation or prosecution; action or complaint, in any other court or place whatsoever."

Article 17 (now Article 15) provided that the power of suspending laws was solely within the province of the legislature. Article 19 (now Article 17) guaranteed that martial law would be applied only to those in the army or "militia in active service."

The convention adopted other changes to specific articles that were designed to clarify language. For example, in Articles 6 and 20 (now Articles 6 and 18) was incorporated the phrase "in a legal way." Other phrases inserted in other articles were "by their legal representatives" and "in a constitutional manner." Elections were to be without corruption, and trial by jury was to be a matter of right "when an issue in fact proper for the cognizance of a jury, is joined in a court of law."

The council also proposed, and the convention refused to adopt, prohibition against an ex post facto law, although it is not clear from any record now available

[8] Ibid., 58.

why the convention objected to such a proposal. In any case, no ex post facto article has ever been adopted in Vermont. Ultimately, Article 1, Section 10 of the United States Constitution effectively incorporated a prohibition against ex post facto laws into states' constitutions.

The most important addition to Chapter 2 was the separation of powers clause. Neither the Vermont Constitution of 1777 nor the model Pennsylvania Constitution of 1776 contained such a clause. Again, the numerous instances of the legislature delegating to itself matters that were traditionally within the purview of the judiciary led to the inclusion of this clause. Other sections of the constitution were revised to conform to this new section.

A new section was also added to strengthen the court's powers in matters best reserved to the judiciary. It prohibited the legislature from declaring any person "guilty of treason or felony."

The last section added to the constitution prohibited forfeitures of the property of suicides. It also included the following sentence: "Nor shall any article which shall accidentally occasion the death of any person be henceforth deemed a deodand [forfeit], or in any way forfeited, on account of such misfortune." The origin of this section remains a mystery, and the section remains in Vermont's present constitution (sec. 65).

In addition to the insertion of whole new sections into the constitution, many changes were made to existing sections. The convention agreed that tenure during good behavior should be changed. Judges were now to be elected annually instead of being permitted to continue in office on the basis of poorly defined "good behavior." The title of deputy-governor was changed to lieutenant-governor. The council also suggested that the legislature should be able to expel a member "but not for causes known to their constituents antecedent to their election." The convention accepted the proposal. Previously the representatives could expel a member, but not a second time for the same cause.

The representatives were now to be limited in their authority to administer oaths or affirmations to matters depending before them. The Constitution of 1777 had permitted them to administer oaths or affirmations on examination of witnesses. The word "I" in oaths to be taken by all public officials or by freemen was changed to "you." A single member of the House of Representatives was now given the right to demand the "yeas and nays" on any question; formerly, one-third of the members were required to demand the yeas and nays.

The process of reviewing bills by the governor and his council was amended, as was the obligation of all inhabitants, not just freemen, to complete military training. Another amendment authorized awarding of costs in impeachment trials. Such a provision was not included in the 1777 Constitution.

Interestingly enough, although the Continental Congress had repeatedly stalled any effort on the part of Vermont to become a member of that body, both the constitutions of 1777 and 1786 made provisions for the election of delegates from Vermont to the Congress. The provisions, of course, were deleted as unnecessary from the 1793 Constitution because Vermont had by then been admitted into the Union, and election to Congress was determined by federal law.

Bail was to be available and not to be excessive for all prisoners except those charged with capital offenses. The 1786 Constitution, further, denied bail as a matter of right to prisoners in execution of sentence. Since many populated areas of the state had not yet been officially organized and declared towns, it was necessary to designate an office for the filing of deeds. The county clerk's office was designated for this purpose. The revised constitution ensured that all "persons" of good character would be deemed entitled to all the rights of a native Vermonter, except that two years' residency was required for election to certain state offices. Formerly no residency was required of citizens, or "Freemen"; only "foreigners" had to reside for two years in the state before they could be elected.

The 1786 Constitution added a new duty to the Council of Censors, "to inquire whether the constitution has been preserved inviolate in every part during the last septenary; (including the year of their service)." The council was also given subpoena powers. This latter provision came about because of the inability of the council to obtain records necessary to do their work properly.

Between the meeting of the Council of Censors in 1785 and 1792, Vermont was admitted as the fourteenth state of the United States of America. This led the 1792 council to suggest the elimination or amending of those sections of the 1786 Constitution alluding to membership in the Continental Congress. The convention accomplished this. The preamble to the Constitution of 1777 contained a lengthy diatribe against the evils of the state of New York, but the convention deleted the preamble once Vermont had been admitted to the Union and the two states were on an equal basis.

The framers of the Constitution of 1777 also inserted a clause in the oath taken by members of the General Assembly, in which each representative declared:

> I do believe in one God, the Creator and Governor of the Universe, the rewarder of the good and punisher of the wicked. And I do acknowledge the scriptures of the old and new testaments to be given by divine inspiration, and own and profess the protestant religion.

The Pennsylvania model had contained a similar provision, but it had not included the final clause professing the Protestant religion. The convention adopted the council's proposal that the Constitution of 1793 contain no preferred religion provision. Indeed, the 1793 Constitution contains no religious qualification at all.

For the first time, the Council of Censors recommended to the convention of 1793 that a Senate replace the Governor's Council. This suggestion was not adopted by this convention.

The journal of the 1793 convention that met to consider the redrafted constitution recommended by the Council of Censors showed the members of that convention to be a contentious group. Although they agreed on the provisions of Chapter 1 with one minor change, they were unable to agree on the new Chapter 2. Not being able to arrive at any semblance of unanimity on that chapter, they appointed a committee to work out a new constitution that would be agreeable to the members. The committee reported to the convention and recommended that the 1786 Constitution be adopted "in bulk" with a few changes.

The constitution adopted by the convention of 1793 remains the basic document. Amendments to the state's constitution are always amendments to the Constitution of 1793.

Among the small changes made by the convention were the following: funds were to be appropriated only by the legislature, and the treasurer could not disburse funds without such authorization; to be elected a representative a candidate must have resided in the state for at least two years and in the town from which elected the last year; the seal of the state was to be kept by the governor instead of by the council; impeachment was not to be a bar to a "prosecution at law"; and four years' residence was required before one could run for governor. Other changes were related to style and precision in language, such as the use of the plural where appropriate, or changing words for better emphasis and clarity.

With the adoption of the Constitution of 1793, the first chapter of the constitutional history of Vermont came to a close. In the years between 1777 and 1793 Vermont had declared its independence; acted as a nation; staved off all enemies, domestic and foreign; joined the Union; and, after much trial and error, adopted its basic constitution. The second chapter commenced with a stable, growing state and ended with the demise of the Council of Censors.

THE COUNCIL OF CENSORS

Every septenary a Council of Censors of thirteen men was elected by the population at large to determine, among other duties, whether the constitution should be amended. The council was not required to recommend amendments each septenary, but it was the only group authorized by the constitution to recommend changes. The council could not, by itself, adopt its recommended amendments: it had to call a convention to accept or reject its recommendations. The convention, on the other hand, was not empowered by the constitution to initiate any amendments on its own.

Neither the third Council of Censors, which met in 1799, nor the fourth council, which met in 1806, proposed any amendments to the constitution. The fifth Council of Censors, meeting in 1813, did submit twenty-eight recommendations of amendments to the convention called to consider these suggestions. One of these recommendations was to replace the Governor's Council with a Senate. Adoption of this recommendation would have brought Vermont's frame of government in line with the bicameral legislatures of the federal government and the rest of the states. The recommendation was a renewal of one offered by the council of 1792 and rejected by the convention of 1793.

To the statement of proposals contained in their address to the convention, the fifth council appended material to persuade the convention to adopt the recommendation establishing a Senate. This consisted of extracts from lectures delivered by James Wilson, a signatory of the U.S. Constitution and a former justice of the U.S. Supreme Court, in 1790, 1791, and 1792, before, to quote the Council, "the rage of party spirit was known in the country."

This appeal would suggest that the state of Vermont, in 1813, was torn by political party strife. Vermont at the close of the eighteenth century had seen the approaching demise of the Federalist party and the rise of the Jeffersonian Republicans. During the War of 1812, however, there was a resurgence of the old Federalist spirit, which at times led to violent party strife, generated by the prohibition against trade with Canada, one of Vermont's principal trading partners, and by the results of the British blockade of the East Coast ports. There were those Vermonters who wanted to continue the fight against Great Britain and those who for economic reasons opposed the war. The censors hoped that reason, rather than emotion or party, would prevail during the convention.

The convention that met to consider the recommendations, however, rejected all twenty-eight. It summarily dismissed twenty-six. Only two of the proposals submitted were deemed important enough to warrant discussion and rejection by ballot. The establishment of the Senate to replace the Governor's Council would have to await a future date.

The next council met in 1820. It did not again propose that a Senate be substituted for the Governor's Council. Instead it suggested that the Governor's Council be abolished and the governor become the sole executive. In all it offered five proposals of amendment. In addition to the abolition of the Governor's Council, the Council of Censors proposed that the House of Representatives be reappointed on the basis of population (one representative for every 2,000 people) instead of territory (one representative for every town). It also suggested a seven-year term for judges rather than annual elections, as called for by the 1793 Constitution. These two recommendations foreshadowed changes to come about a century and a half later. The convention rejected all five recommendations. Since the adoption of the Constitution of 1793, thirty-three recommendations of amendment had been proposed by four Councils of Censors, and none had been adopted by the conventions.

The censors of 1827 proposed three amendments. The convention adopted one and rejected two. The Constitution of 1793 was not rewritten. Amendments, denoted "articles," were added and numbered consecutively. The first amendment to the Vermont Constitution was designated Article 1. (It has been amended further and is now Section 42.) Redefining the qualifications for citizenship in Vermont, it declared:

> No person, who is not already a freeman of this state, shall be entitled to exercise the privileges of a freeman, unless he be a natural born citizen of this, or some one of the United States or until he shall have been naturalized agreeably to the acts of Congress.

Prior to this amendment, residence in Vermont for one year was the only requirement for becoming a citizen of the state. Now, in addition to the residence requirement, one could become a citizen of Vermont through native birth, prior citizenship, or naturalization; in effect, U.S. citizenship became a prerequisite for Vermont citizenship, and foreigners not willing to become American citizens were prohibited from enjoying the benefits of freemen (citizens) of Vermont.

From its inception as an independent nation in the eighteenth century, Vermont had enjoyed a steady growth in population. In the early nineteenth century, however, this growth dwindled. The opening of the Northwest Territory for settlement greatly attracted settlers from the Northeast, and many Vermonters emigrated west, even though Vermont itself was still a frontier with much open land available for settlement. This exodus was offset in part by an influx of immigrants from Canada and Europe. The first amendment to the Constitution of Vermont was passed to force these immigrants to become American citizens.

Just as young Vermonters left during this period for new frontiers in the West that appeared more attractive than the native hills of Vermont, they later left because of the attraction of better paying jobs in industry in other states. Vermont never developed an industrial society. It had remained agrarian and politically conservative and became known for its slowness to change, which was also evident in its unwillingness to change its constitution quickly.

Major changes in the constitution thus did not appear until the 1834 Council of Censors (eighth) again proposed the elimination of the Governor's Council, and again substituted the Senate as a second branch of the legislature. The convention of 1836 considered twenty proposals of amendment and adopted twelve, but the most far-reaching, of course, was the institution of the bicameral legislature, with the adoption of the Senate as the second branch.

The convention retained the House of Representatives as "the most numerous branch of the Legislature" (Article 2). Article 3 vested the legislative power in a Senate and House of Representatives to be called "the General Assembly of the State of Vermont." The two bodies were to have equal power, but revenue bills had to originate in the House (the Senate could, however, amend). The composition of the Senate was set at thirty members, one from each county, and the balance apportioned to the counties according to population (Article 4). The method of their election was set out in Article 5. The next article defined the powers of the Senate, designating the lieutenant-governor as its president and presiding officer.

Article 7 empowered the Senate to try impeachments; Article 8 established the executive power solely in the governor, and the Governor's Council was abolished. Because of the establishment of the Senate and the elimination of the Governor's Council, revisions of Sections 9, 10, and 16 of the constitution were necessary. Amendments designated as Articles 9, 10, and 11 accomplished these changes.

Section 9 of the Constitution of 1793 had given the Governor's Council joint powers with the House of Representatives in the direct election of certain other state officials. Articles 9 and 10 substituted the Senate in place of the Governor's Council. Section 10 of the constitution had given certain powers relative to the election of the governor, lieutenant-governor, and treasurer to the House of Representatives and the Governor's Council. Section 16 designated the powers of the governor and council in the adoption or rejection of bills passed by the General Assembly, and Article 11 eliminated the council from its provisions. Through Article 12, the writ of habeas corpus became a constitutional right; adopted by the convention of 1836, it was now "a writ, issuable of right; and the General Assembly shall make provision to render it a speedy and effectual remedy in all cases proper therefor."

Finally, Article 13 was adopted, which disposed of superseded parts of the constitution. Vermont had now joined the rest of the nation with a bicameral legislature.

Among the proposals from the Council of Censors of 1834 rejected by the convention of 1836 was one that would have authorized the election of certain local officials by the freemen of their districts rather than by the General Assembly. A septenary later the Council of Censors of 1841 submitted ten proposals of amendment, again including one that would have allowed local freemen to elect local officials. The censors also renewed their proposal that judges be elected for a seven-year term. They requested an amendment setting the term for senators at three years, with one-third to be elected each year. They proposed that elections be held in October instead of September and that the legislature convene in January instead of October. For the first time it was recommended that a statewide referendum be conducted to consider all proposals of amendment. The convention rejected all ten proposals.

In 1848 the Council of Censors renewed its recommendation that the freemen of a district elect their local officials. The convention of 1850 agreed to this recommendation and devoted several articles to describing the manner of their election.

Article 14 provided for the election of the assistant judges of the county court by the freemen of their counties. The office of assistant judge was not new to the states in the nation; in Vermont, however, the office had never been dignified by inclusion in the constitution. The assistant judges were, in effect, county commissioners who had judicial duties. They sat with the judges elected by the General Assembly. The jurisdiction of the assistant judges was limited to matters filed in the county from which they had been elected. There were no legal qualifications for the position of assistant judge. These judges were not unique to Vermont in 1850, but since then all states except Vermont have abolished the position.

Article 15 called for the election of sheriffs and high bailiffs by the freemen of their counties. Article 16 provided for local elections of state's attorneys; judges of probate were to be elected by freemen of their districts (Article 17). Article 18 provided for the election of justices of the peace by the freemen of their towns. This article also prescribed the formula for determining the number of justices of the peace in each town. Article 19 limited terms of office of the locally elected officials to one year. Article 20 directed their election "at the times and in the manner now directed in the Constitution for the choice of Senators."

Provision was made for the legislature to declare who should succeed the governor or lieutenant-governor in case of a vacancy in either office. The governor was given the power to appoint a state treasurer if the office became vacant (Article 21). The state treasurer, sheriffs, and high bailiffs were now to be required to give security to their constituents "in such manner and in such sums as shall be directed by the Legislature" (Article 22). The next article (23) refined Article 4 of the amendments, which delineated the number, qualification, and apportionment of the Senate. The convention of 1850 rejected a renewed proposal to reapportion the House of Representatives on the basis of population.

Here the political power of the small towns was evident. Towns of 50 inhabitants enjoyed the same voting power in the House of Representatives as towns with a population of 5000; and because there were many more small towns than large towns, no reapportionment was possible. It was not until the United States Supreme Court ruled that districts must be based on numbers rather than territory ("one man, one vote") that Vermont reapportioned its House of Representatives.

Although the constitution granted to the Council of Censors the power to call a convention to consider its recommendation of amendments to the constitution, no direction was given as to the number or qualifications of delegates to the convention. The only direction to the Council of Censors was contained in Section 42 (now revoked):

> The said Council of Censors shall also have power to call a Convention, to meet within two years after their sitting, if there appears to them an absolute necessity of amending any article of the Constitution, which may be defective—explaining so much as may be thought not clearly expressed—and adding such as are necessary for the preservation of the rights and happiness of the people; but the articles to be

amended, and the amendments proposed, and such articles as are to be proposed to be added or abolished, shall be promulgated at least six months before the day appointed for the election of such Convention, for the previous consideration of the people, that they may have an opportunity of instructing their delegates on the subject.

Like the House of Representatives, each convention called by the previous Councils of Censors had been composed of one delegate from each town in the state. When the Council of 1855 ordered a convention to consider nineteen proposals of amendment, it limited the number of delegates to ninety, significantly reducing their number. In 1855 there were 240 towns.

One can only speculate on the reasons for this reduction in convention delegates. The minutes of the council's meetings offer no clues. The council, moreover, not certain of its authority to limit the number of delegates to the convention, proposed that the constitution be amended to permit a convention composed of ninety delegates.

This convention of ninety delegates not only refused to consider that proposal of amendment but also refused to consider any of the other proposals submitted by the council of 1855. It was the position of the convention that it had been illegally convened because it was not composed of a delegate from each town, as had every previous convention.

Among the rejected proposals was a recommendation to change the term of senators, who were elected annually, to four years, and to allow each county two senators. This proposal has never been adopted.

Three of the rejected proposals are of particular interest. One would have had the secretary of state and the auditor of accounts elected by the freemen. Another would have required biennial sessions of the General Assembly instead of annual sessions. A third would have limited membership in the House of Representatives to 150 and given the General Assembly the power to create representative districts. Although these three proposals were not considered by the convention of 1857, all are now incorporated into the Vermont Constitution. all are now incorporated into the Vermont Constitution.

The next council (the twelfth) made no recommendation of amendments. No convention was called.

The Council of Censors elected in 1869 recommended their own demise. But why should a procedure for amending the constitution that had existed since the formation of the state be abandoned and a new system substituted? The answers lie in the reports of the minority and majority of a committee established by the council to explore that question. The minority report favored the new amendment procedure; the minority members, while agreeing that the convention system of amendment was the best in 1777, stated:

Then but very few newspapers, if any, existed in the State; but few books; our free schools were extremely limited in their means to impart education to the rising generation, and it is not to become a wonder that the leaders of that day considered it unsafe, or at least not best, to trust the amending of the Constitution in the hands of the people directly.[9]

The report continued by reminding the council that Vermont had been the only state to adopt the Pennsylvania model of constitutional amendment. It noted that even Pennsylvania had long ago discarded that system.

It added that the people knew and understood little and cared less about their constitution and how it was amended. The report raised the question, "Is it best or expedient to perpetuate and continue a system so little understood, and in which so little interest is manifested?"[10]

It was the view of the minority that the people should have a part in amending their basic document. These minority members felt that their fellow citizens in 1869 were more intelligent, better informed, and better educated than their forbears, and could be trusted: "They are capable of self-government, and it is eminently proper and in accordance with republican principles and democratic ideas to suffer the people to manage and control their own political affairs in their own way."[11]

The minority report also described the political dichotomy that existed during the early years of statehood. The report recalled that the Federalists had not trusted the people, but the Republicans had, and although the Federalists had disappeared, the relic of old Federal rule remained. Finally, noting that the other duties of the council had withered away and that no legislative reviews had been done in recent years, the minority report concluded by asking the Council of Censors to let the question of the process of amendment be decided by the people through a convention ordered by the council.

The majority report was a rebuttal to the report of the minority. It pointed out:

> Our Constitution was framed for the whole people. It is the organic law which governs not *municipalities* but *the people* of municipalities, and as such, ought to be beyond the reach of municipalities to control. The Council, as now constituted, are elected by *the people*, on a general ticket; and a small town with one hundred voters cannot neutralize the voice of a town with ten thousand inhabitants in selecting the council. Theoretically, then, the Council created by the people themselves more emphatically represents the popular voice than any other tribunal in our frame of government.[12]

[9] Ibid., 659.
[10] Ibid., 659.
[11] Ibid., 660.
[12] Ibid., 683.

The majority also argued that the other powers delegated to the council acted as a check over the different departments of government, but they agreed with the minority that the matter should go to the convention for decision.

THE TEN-YEAR TIME LOCK

The convention, having decided that the time had passed for the Council of Censors, eliminated it and set up a legislative referendum with a ten-year time lock. As finally adopted, the amending process consisted of introduction through the Senate, which had to approve the proposal by a two-thirds vote; then the House had to approve the amendments by a majority of votes taken that session; and finally, at the next General Assembly, the Senate and the House had to pass the proposals by a majority. Provision was made for publication of the proposals in the principal newspapers in the state. Once approval had been properly attained, the proposals were to be submitted to a direct vote by the freemen of the state and required a majority of those votes to be adopted and become part of the constitution. It was also provided that these proposals could only be introduced "at the session of the General Assembly of this State, A.D. 1880, and at the session thereof every tenth year thereafter" (Article of Amendment 25, since revoked). Thus, the ten-year time lock was established.

The adoption of Article 26 of the amendments in 1870 abolished the Council of Censors. During their existence, 107 proposals were submitted to and considered by conventions. Only twenty-six were adopted and included in the constitution.

In establishing the ten-year time lock, the intent of the convention was to ensure the stability of the constitution. However, in 1880, the first year that amendments could be proposed, twenty-three were submitted for consideration. Some were perennials, such as the proposal to hold elections in November and open sessions of the legislature in January (again rejected). Another perennial was the proposal to limit the number of representatives to 150. Other proposals were relatively new.

In 1890 no amendments were adopted, although nine were proposed. Among those rejected was a proposal to reorganize the court system and one enabling the Senate to propose constitutional amendments at any session. Senators, by one proposal, would be apportioned by population, and they and the representatives would have four-year terms. It was proposed that representatives be apportioned to districts. It will be seen that perseverance would eventually lead to the adoption of these proposals in some form.

In 1900 four proposals of amendment were introduced. All were rejected by one or both bodies of the General Assembly.

In 1910, of fifteen proposals of amendment, eight were adopted. Two proposals on amending the constitution were rejected, as was a proposal for female suffrage. Another proposal was rejected which would have established a ten-year tem for the judges of the supreme court. A change was also proposed to the Bill of Rights: that the condemnation article be changed from "use" and "uses" to "benefit" or "benefits," or that "or benefits" be added after the words "public uses." It was the first proposed change to the Bill of Rights since the adoption of the 1793 Constitution. It was rejected.

The recommendation to change the meeting date of the General Assembly was finally adopted by the freemen in 1913. Now sessions would commence on the first Wednesday after the first Monday in January, beginning in 1915. Heretofore sessions had been held biennially in even years, and the last session had been held in 1912. This amendment became Article 30 of the amendments. This new article also provided for the election of named officers biennially, commencing in November 1914.

Under the new election procedure, all persons who had been elected in 1912 to offices set out in the article were to hold office until the term of their successors commenced. Judges were the forgotten persons. The judges of the supreme and county courts were not elected by the freemen but by the General Assembly. In 1912 they received commissions from the governor, with terms of office designated to a fixed day. Governor Allen Fletcher requested advice of the supreme court as to whether, after the expiration of the commission, he could appoint new judges for vacancies.

The court, through the chief justice, agreed that the governor could appoint as he would if a vacancy existed, issuing a new commission for two years. Traditionally, the legislature had reelected all sitting judges. Governor Fletcher, rejecting tradition, did not reappoint two supreme court judges and one county court judge.

When the legislature met on January 15, the new time established by the last amendment to the constitution, an impasse occurred: the General Assembly passed a resolution establishing a date for the election of judges, but a new governor was now in office, and the new governor did not immediately sign the resolution. The impasse was resolved by the actions of the judges, who met and unanimously submitted their resignations to the governor. The governor then signed the resolution. At this point, the legislature reversed Governor Fletcher's action and reinstituted the judges of the previous bench.

As a sidelight, Chief Justice John Rowell, of the supreme court which had issued the advisory opinion (for which there was no authority), had retired and been elected president of the Vermont Bar Association. He eventually came to be instrumental in persuading the bar to support the legislature in repudiating his own opinion.

The arrangement of the constitution had never been changed. All amendments were addenda to the original document. By 1910 twenty-eight articles of amendment had been adopted. In 1913 the freemen adopted an additional eight.

One of these, Article 36, authorized the judges of the supreme court (designated as "justices" in Article 34 to

> revise Chapter 2 of the constitution by incorporating into said chapter all amendments of the constitution that are now or may be then in force and excluding therefrom all sections, clauses and words not in force and rearranging and renumbering the sections thereof under appropriate titles as in their judgment may be most logical and convenient; and said revised Chapter 2 as certified to the secretary of state by said judges or a majority thereof shall be a part of the constitution of this state in substitution for existing Chapter 2 and all amendments thereof.

Finally, the constitution would be a single document.

In 1921 there were twenty-one proposals of amendment, only four of which were adopted. Women's suffrage was one (following the Seventeenth Amendment to the United States Constitution). Two of those adopted amended articles of Chapter 1: Article 1 of Chapter 1 was amended by placing both men and women on the same footing as to the age limit (twenty-one) when they could be held to servitude or apprenticeship without their consent (the 1793 Constitution placed the age for females at eighteen and for males at twenty-one). Article 10 of Chapter 1 was amended to permit a person accused of a crime not punishable by "death or imprisonment in the state's prison [felony]" to waive his right to a trial. The last amendment enabled the General Assembly to enact laws regulating the mode of filling vacancies in the House of Representatives.

In 1931 seven amendments were proposed. All were rejected. The four proposals in 1941 met the same fate. In 1951 the climate changed: three proposals of amendment were offered, and all three were adopted. In 1961 eight proposals were submitted; only one was adopted.

In 1970 a bill was introduced into the Senate that called for a referendum on holding a constitutional convention limited to considering four almost perennial amendments. The bill never got to the floor of the Senate for debate; after all, the next session of the legislature would convene in less than a year, at which time the ten-year time lock permitted amendments to be introduced.

However, the General Assembly had appointed a Constitutional Commission, which submitted an interim report in 1969 and a final report in 1971. It was from this report that most of the proposed amendments originated. Nine proposals were submitted to the Senate. It merged the first and second proposals. The new proposal would establish four-year terms for certain officials.

As in previous years, it became the most controversial proposal. The legislature approved this amendment in the 1971 and 1973 sessions. The people of Vermont were satisfied with the two-year term for governor and other state officials and, at the referendum, refused to concur. Vermont still has a two-year term for governor, lieutenant-governor, treasurer, secretary of state, auditor of accounts, and attorney general.

The third proposal reduced the time lock for constitutional amendments to each biennial session. The proposal was amended to a four-year time lock, and the General Assembly concurred. It was adopted by a referendum of the people of Vermont, as the constitution required, and remains as the time in which amendments can be proposed today.

The fourth proposal, concerning allocation of highway funds, was referred to a committee in the Senate. The committee never released it.

The next proposal led to a far-reaching revision of the judicial system. The Constitution of 1793 had established the separation of the judicial branch from the legislative and executive branches, and had defined the judicial branch in a short section in Chapter 2. The organization and functions of the judicial branch were left to the legislature, and through that process, in 1870, the judges (who came to be called justices in 1913) would be elected biennially.

The new proposal sought to revise the judicial branch by vesting the judicial power in a "unified judicial system which shall be composed of a Supreme Court, a Superior Court and such other *subordinate* Courts as the General Assembly may from time to time ordain or establish." The supreme court would be composed of a chief justice and four associate justices, and its jurisdiction would include administrative control of the courts of the state and disciplinary authority over judges and attorneys.

The proposal also defined the jurisdiction of the subordinate courts. It created a procedure for filling vacancies in the judicial ranks through appointment by the governor from a list of nominees determined by a judicial nominating body established by the General Assembly. The appointee was to be confirmed by the Senate, and the term of office was now fixed at six years. At the end of each six-year term, the General Assembly would vote to retain the justice or judge.

The supreme court was granted rule-making power governing the administration of the courts, and governing practice and procedure in civil and criminal cases. These rules, however, could be revised by the General Assembly. The proposal included mandatory retirement for justices at the age of seventy and stipulated that, in the exercise of its disciplinary power, the supreme court would be authorized to suspend any justice or judge.

There was little discussion of these sweeping reforms, and they were adopted by the citizens' referendum in 1974.

The voting age was reduced from twenty-one to eighteen, conforming to the federal constitution.

Finally, the House of Representatives reapportioned itself. Instead of one representative for each town, there would now be 150 representatives. The state would be organized into districts, but no more than two representatives would be allowed per district. Here again the legislature followed the United States Supreme Court. A provision for preferential taxation on agricultural land was rejected.

Under the new four-year time lock, the next biennial session at which amendments could be proposed was the session of 1975, at which five proposals were submitted. None were adopted.

It is now over a hundred years since Article 25 was adopted, the Council of Censors was eliminated, and the constitution's earliest structuring period ended. The only changes in the body of the constitution, other than the articles of amendment themselves, were those permitted by the Vermont Supreme Court pursuant to authorization by Article of Amendment 36. This occurred in 1913. The court was authorized to revise Chapter 2 by

> incorporating into said Chapter all amendments of the Constitution that are now or may be then in force and excluding therefrom all sections, clauses and words not in force and rearranging and renumbering the sections thereof under appropriate titles as in their judgment may be most logical and convenient; and said revised Chapter II as certified to the Secretary of State by said Justices or a majority thereof shall be a part of the Constitution of this State in substitution for existing Chapter II and all amendments thereof.

The Supreme Courts of 1913 and 1974 revised Chapter 2.

In 1979 eight proposals were considered by the Senate; of these, only one was adopted. It redefined "bail" and is now Article of Amendment 49. In 1983, of ten amendments proposed, only one, providing for the reapportionment of the legislature following each federal decennial census (Article of Amendment 50), was adopted. Of the six 1987 proposals none was adopted.

Since the adoption of the constitution in 1793 107 proposals have been submitted to conventions by the Council of Censors, of which 26 were adopted. during the ten-year time lock period, there were 104 proposals, of which 22 were adopted. Since the advent of the four-year time lock, of 29 proposals, 2 have been adopted. Today the constitution has remained unamended for almost a decade. With few substantive changes, it has remained a simple document for over 200 years.

SUMMARY

Three constitutions have governed the State of Vermont; the last was ratified in 1793. Since then 50 amendments have been adopted, only two of which affected provisions of the Declaration of Rights contained in Chapter 1 of the 1793 Constitution, which remains the basic Vermont constitution.

In 1913 and 1974 the Vermont Supreme Court, by authority of Article of Amendment 36 adopted in 1913, revised Chapter 2 of the constitution to, in "all sections, clauses and words not in force and rearranging and renumbering the sections thereof under appropriate titles as in their judgment may be most logical and convenient."

The present constitution must be read as Chapter 1, not changed in any way by any authority except by amendments, and as Chapter 2, last revised in 1974 as certified to the Secretary of State by the Vermont Supreme Court of that year. One must then look for Articles of Amendment numbers 49 and 50 to complete the document.

The full text of the constitution is found in the *Vermont Statutes Annotated* published by Equity Publishing Company. It is also contained in a pamphlet published by the Secretary of State of Vermont in 1991. Although there are slight differences between the two publications, they are not substantive.

Vermont's constitution is a short document representing the convictions of its people. Chapter 1 is a statement of the fundamental rights of its citizens. It is significant that this Declaration of Rights precedes the Frame of Government contained in Chapter 2. Substance is more important than form.

The constitution has never been amended by convention called in any way except as required by the various Councils of Censors. It is not a document that may be amended quickly. A septenary, then ten-year, then four-year requirement has always forced Vermonters to deliberate before any changes could be made. Nor do the citizens always follow the suggestions of their general assembly. They have rejected provisions lenghtening the terms of their state officials. Although the State approved the Equal Rights Amendment to the U.S. Constitution, the citizens of Vermont rejected such an amendment to their own constitution.

PART TWO

The Vermont Constitution and Commentary

In *State v. Badger* (1982), the Vermont Supreme Court, writing through the author, said:

> Our first concern is comity between this court and the United States Supreme Court. We stand on a different footing when we evaluate federal constitutional claims. On federal issues, we are no more than an intermediate court, attempting to apply the "supreme law of the land," as pronounced by the United States Supreme Court. Supreme Court authority over our federal rulings is absolute. Yet, if our ruling is based on an adequate and independent state ground, federal review is limited to a determination of whether Vermont law violates some provision of federal law . . . fulfillment of this court's responsibilities as a member of the Federalist system requires us to consider the availability of state grounds before federal appeal.
>
> The institutional concern is buttressed by an even weightier consideration: the authority of the Vermont Constitution itself. The Vermont Constitution is the fundamental charter of our state, and it is this Court's duty to enforce the constitution. Although the Vermont and federal constitutions "have a common origin and a similar purpose our constitution is not a mere reflection of the federal charter. Historically and textually, it differs from the United States Constitution. It predates the federal counterpart, as it extends back to Vermont's fundamental law" (citations omitted).

Further in the same case, the court said, "We are free, of course, to provide more generous protection to rights under the Vermont Constitution than afforded by the federal charter"; and also, "If our state constitution is to mean anything, it must be enforced where it is the only law capable of providing a final answer to a claim, and a party, such as this defendant, has invoked its protections."

Later, in *State v. Jewett* (1985), Justice Thomas Hayes wrote:

> This occasion makes clear the need to raise the plane of consciousness about the resurgence of federalism that is sweeping across the country. Since 1970 there have been over 250 cases in which state appellate courts have viewed the scope of rights under state constitutions as broader than those secured by the federal constitution as interpreted by the United States Supreme Court.

He then outlined various approaches to state constitutional arguments such as historical, textual, and economic, as well as sister state approaches and approaches involving social materials.

The present Vermont Supreme Court has shown no hesitancy in following *Badger* and *Jewett*. In January 1991, in *State v. Kirchoff*, the court rejected the "open field" doctrine enunciated in *Oliver v. United States* (1984), saying, "We now hold that a lawful possessor may claim privacy in 'open fields' under Article II of the Vermont Constitution, where indicia would lead a reasonable person to conclude that the area is private."

1 A Declaration of the Rights of the Inhabitants of the State of Vermont

Article 1

Declaration of Natural Rights; Prohibition of Slavery

That all men are born equally free and independent, and have certain natural, inherent, and unalienable rights, amongst which are the enjoying and defending life and liberty, acquiring, possessing and protecting property, and pursuing and obtaining happiness and safety; therefore no person born in this country, or brought from over sea, ought to be holden by law, to serve any person as a servant, slave or apprentice, after he arrives to the age of twenty-one years, unless he is bound by his own consent, after he arrives to such age, or bound by law for the payment of debts, damages, fines, costs, or the like.

The first clause of this article, ending with "safety," comes directly from the Pennsylvania Constitution of 1776 and was incorporated into Vermont's first constitution in 1777. The second clause, however, was written into the 1777 Constitution by the Vermonters at the Windsor Convention. It represents the first constitutional statement prohibiting slavery in any of the original state constitutions.

The "certain natural, inherent, and unalienable rights" are subject to limitations. In *Lincoln v. Smith* (1855) the Vermont Supreme Court declared: "This article seems to be a recitation of some of the natural rights of men before entering into the social compact. But these rights may be controlled or modified by the laws of the land. In the language of Judge Blackstone, 'they are absolute and inherent rights without any control, or diminution; save only by the laws of the land.'" The natural rights doctrine, it would seem, is absolute only to the extent that it is not modified by law. The court further stated that "neither the first nor the ninth articles should be so construed as to trammel the legislature in passing such laws as they shall deem the public good requires; although such laws may act upon and abridge the natural rights of persons before entering into the social compact."

In *State v. Harrington* (1896) the court stated:

> "Rights of property, like all other social and conventional rights, are subject to such reasonable limitations in their enjoyment as shall prevent them from being injurious, and to such reasonable restraints and regulations established by law, as the legislature, under the governing and controlling power vested in it by the constitution, may think necessary and expedient." The power we allude to is the police power, the power vested in the legislature by the constitution to make, ordain and establish all manner of wholesome and reasonable laws, statutes and ordinances, either with penalties, or without, not repugnant to the constitution, as it shall judge to be for the welfare of the commonwealth, and of the subjects of the same. (C. J. Shaw in *Commonwealth v. Alger*, 7 Cush. 53).

Further, the court quoted Chief Justice Redfield, who, in *Thorpe v. R. & B. R. Co.* (1854), stated the proposition in these terms:

> This police power of the state extends to the protection of the lives, limbs, health, comfort and quiet of all persons, and the protection of all property within the state . . . it must of course be within the range of legislative action to define the mode and manner in which every one may so use his own not to injure others.

The antislavery clause of the 1777 Vermont Constitution made a distinction in age between males and females. Males were to be considered free at age twenty-one, while females' age of majority was set at eighteen. Article of Amendment 34, adopted in 1924, eliminated the gender distinction, making males and females free at age twenty-one.

Although slavery was abolished in Vermont in 1777, nevertheless persons purporting to be slaves were present in Vermont. The first census of the United States in 1790 noted sixteen slaves in Vermont. Yet in 1786 the Vermont legislature found it necessary to pass an act entitled "An act to prevent the sale and transportation of Negroes and Mulattoes out of this State." The preamble says it all:

> "Whereas, by the constitution of this State, all the subjects of this commonwealth, of whatever color, are equally entitled to the inestimable blessings of freedom, unless they have forfeited the same by the commission of some crime; and the idea of slavery is expressly and totally exploded from our free government.
>
> And whereas, instances have happened of the former owners of negro slaves in this commonwealth, making sale of such persons as slaves, notwithstanding their being liberated by the Constitution; and attempts been made to transport such persons to foreign parts, in open violation of the laws of the land.

Later, in 1802, the town of Windsor brought an action to recover support of an aged black woman who was, it was alleged, the slave of the defendant (*Windsor v. Jacob*, 1802).The town further alleged that the defendant had purchased her in 1783 and had kept her in slavery until she was too old to work, at which time he forced her to leave his home and she became a charge on the town. To prove the allegation of slavery, the plaintiff offered as evidence a bill of sale showing that the defendant had purchased one Dinah White, a black slave, whom he brought into the town of Windsor. The defendant objected to the introduction of the document.

The court said:

> The question must turn upon the validity or operative force of this instrument within this State. If the bill of sale could by our Constitution operate to bind the woman in slavery when brought by the defendant to inhabit within this State, then it ought to be admitted in evidence; and the law will raise a liability in the slave holder to maintain her through all the vicissitudes of life; but if otherwise it is void.
>
> Our State constitution is express, no inhabitant of the State can hold a slave; and though the bill of sale may be binding by the lex loci of another state or dominion, yet when the master becomes an inhabitant of this State his bill of sale ceases to operate here.

The court further held that the state constitution, and not the federal, controlled. As slavery was prohibited by the state constitution, it was held that Dinah White had been free when she entered Vermont in 1783 and was still free. The bill of sale was not allowed in evidence. A footnote to the case: The defendant, Jacob, was a member of the Vermont Supreme Court at this time. He did not sit on the court in this case.

Article 2

Private Property for Public Use; Payment

> That private property ought to be subservient to public uses when necessity requires it, nevertheless, whenever any person's property is taken for the use of the public, the owner ought to receive an equivalent in money.

This article did not appear in the Pennsylvania Constitution of 1776 but was added at Windsor in 1777. Article 2 must be considered in terms of private property, public uses, necessity, taking, and compensation.

PRIVATE PROPERTY AND PUBLIC USE

In *Deerfield River Co. v. Wilmington P. & P. Co.* (1910) the issue of public uses is discussed in some detail. The facts in the case are these: Wilmington Power obtained a charter that permitted it to condemn, when necessary, flowage rights. Provision was made in the charter to determine necessity and damages. Another charter provision required Wilmington Power to furnish, when requested by certain muncipalities, electricity for municipal use and domestic lighting. One of the municipalities made such a request. Such electricity was desirable for lighting the streets of the town of Readsboro. The only way to accomplish this was to erect a dam on the Deerfield River and back the water over Deerfield's land. To do this, Wilmington, in accordance with the power granted in its charter, instituted condemnation proceedings against Deerfield, which contended that the taking would be for a private rather than a public use.

The court first distinguished between a public use and a public benefit. It looked at precedent and stated that "the end to be accomplished must always be the true and ultimate test; and it is quite immaterial that the title and control of the property taken are vested in a private person or corporation, whose actuating motive is private gain." It concluded that "the only use for which the defendant seeks to condemn this land being a public one, the mere fact that its charter powers also embrace matters of private use will not deprive it of this right of condemnation for the public use." The court had already determined, in *Avery v. Vermont Electric Co. et al.* (1903), that a public benefit did satisfy the constitutional demand for a public use.

The court denied to the legislature the right to extend the provisions of the constitution. In *Tyler v. Beacher et al.* (1871) it declared that the attempt by the legislature to exercise the right of eminent domain does not, of itself, settle that it has the right. The question whether the taking was for a public use is one for the courts.

In *Williams v. School District #6* (1860) it was concluded that although public use was to a great extent local, that did not affect the constitutionality of the taking. The use need not be universal. Although confined to a particular district, it may still be public even if some parties benefitted more than others.

The right to use water "for the extinguishment of fires, and for domestic, sanitary and other purposes" restricts the owner to a right for public purposes and not for private purposes. In *In re Barre Water Co.* (1889), commissioners were appointed to assess compensation. The commissioners submitted two amounts to the court, one sum if the water was used only for "extinguishment of fires and for sanitary and domestic use," and a larger sum if used for "all purposes." The Vermont Supreme Court held for the smaller sum. The company had intended to install a large main to supply the village. The surplus water was to be used for light manufacturing. Such use, the court held, would be for a private purpose and could not be gained by eminent domain. In *Snow v. Sandgate* (1894) the Vermont court flatly declared that "the State is not authorized to take private property for private use without the consent of the owner, even by paying therefor an equivalent in money."

NECESSITY

Although the legislature has the power to declare the necessity for the taking of property, the fact of public use can be determined only by the courts (*Tyler v. Beacher et al.* 1871). Any attempt by a legislature to exercise the right of eminent domain does not settle the taking but under the constitution must be settled by the courts.

The question of public use is first a factual one requiring the judiciary to find necessity from the facts. The Vermont legislature had left the matter of the necessity for a public use to be determined by a municipality. The court, in

Stearns et al. v. Barre (1901), stated: "Our constitution in effect declares that private property can be taken by the public only when it is necessary for its use. Of what avail is this constitutional guaranty if there can be no judicial inquiry as to its necessity? The very existence of the provision makes the question of necessity ultimately a judicial one. If it does not the legislature remains supreme in this regard notwithstanding the constitution."

TAKING

What constitutes a taking was first answered in Vermont in the cases of *Foster v. Stafford National Bank* (1884) and *Wead v. St. Johnsbury and Lake Chaplain R. R. Co.* (1891). In *Foster* the court said, "Any injury to the property of an individual which deprives him of the ordinary use of it, is equivalent to a taking, and entitles him to compensation." In *Wead* the railroad company enlarged a highway roadbed as well as building up the roadbed. The court held that building up the roadbed was not a taking, as the landowner was presumably paid when the road was constructed. All additions designed to help the railroad, however, did constitute a taking for which the landowner must be compensated.

When a mill and dam were destroyed to prevent a river from washing out a highway, the person's property was destroyed under the police power of the state to avert imminent public injury and thus was not a taking for which compensation was required (*Aitken v. Wells River*, 1898). A temporary interference with the owners of a mill pond and dam by a municipality by repairing a bridge upstream was not a taking requiring compensation (*East Montpelier v. Wheelock*, 1898). Likewise, raising the grade of a highway less than three feet did not entitle an adjoining property owner to damages, as such activity will be considered repair rather than alteration (*Hoyt v. North Troy*, 1918).

Thus the exercise of police power cannot be construed as the taking of private property for public use. When permits were required and license fees demanded for the installation and operation of certain types of pinball machines, the court in *Sowma v. Parker* (1941) quoted an earlier opinion that "the revocation of the license without a repayment to the licensee of any portion of the sum paid by him for the license infringes no constitutional right, for the license is not a contract but a permit to sell subject to restrictions, and from its very nature is subject to revocation in consequence of a disregard of such restrictions or in the consequence of a change of policy on the part of the government in respect to the exercise of the police power."

A development was instituted by the plaintiffs in the case of *Demers v. Montpelier* (1958). The survey of the development divided the tract into lots located along a forty-foot strip designated as Mountain View Street Extension. The lots were sold to different purchasers. The plaintiffs agreed, in effect, to develop the forty-foot strip in compliance with the requirements of the city of Montpelier necessary to obtain acceptance by the city as a street. They also proposed to lay water and sewer lines. Later the city extended the Mountain View Street Extension but declined to pay compensation to the plaintiffs for the forty-foot strip, claiming no taking as Demers had already dedicated the land as a municipal highway. The court rejected this claim, declaring that such determination by the city was a usurpation of the judicial function. The court then held that the taking of the roadway was a condemnation for public use for which compensation was required.

When a dwelling or other building is declared a nuisance, it may be abated without the payment of compensation as an exercise of the police power. Such action is subject to review by the courts(*Eno v. Burlington*, 1965). However, the state's police power is not unlimited, and when action by the state does permanent physical damage to property to the point of depriving the owner of its beneficial use, that constitutes a taking. Thus where, in salting a road to deice, if the well of the plaintiff was made unfit for drinking, that constitutes a taking for which the owners were entitled to compensation (*Timms v. State*, 1981). Liability does not depend only on a deliberate act but may occur through negligence, as occurred in *Timms and in Griswold v. Weathersfield* (1952). In *Wead v. St. Johnsbury and Lake Champlain R. R. Co.*. the backing up of water by the construction of culverts and embankments, causing injury to adjoining lands, was a taking under this provision of the constitution. Nor can the state claim sovereign immunity (*Makela v. State*, 1964). Nor can a municipality claim compensation from the state when property is held by the municipality in its public, as distinguished from its proprietary, function (*Winooski v. State Highway Board*, 1965).

COMPENSATION

There can be no taking for public use unless compensation is provided for. In *Foster v. Stafford National Bank* (1884) the legislature provided for rights to control gates erected on others' land to control the flow of water. The court held the act unconstitutional because no provision had been made for compensation. The compensation must be in money unless it is agreed otherwise among the parties. There is no exact formula for determining the damages. However, in *Demers v. Montpelier*, the court stated, "In broadest terms, the law measures damage by the market value rule, and awards the landowner the difference between the value of the entire tract before the taking and its value thereafter."

Article 3

Freedom of Religion; Right and Duty of Religious Worship

> That all men have a natural and unalienable right, to worship Almighty God, according to the dicates of their own consciences and understandings, as in their opinion shall be regulated by the word of God; and that no man ought to, or of right can be compelled to attend any religious worship, or erect or support any place of worship, or maintain any minister, contrary to the dictates of his conscience, nor can any man be justly deprived or abridged of any civil right as a citizen, on account of his religious sentiments, or peculia[r] mode of religious worship; and that no authority can, or ought to be vested in, or assumed by, any power whatever, that shall in any case interfere with, or in any manner control the rights of conscience, in the free exercise of religious worship. Nevertheless, every sect or denomination of christians ought to observe the sabbath or Lord's day, and keep up some sort of religious worship, which to them shall seem most agreeable to the revealed will of God.

This article is based on Article II of the Declaration of Rights of Pennsylvania. However, Vermont did not slavishly adopt the Pennsylvania Declaration of Rights verbatim. The committee had reviewed and revised the declaration and in the July convention at Windsor we can assume that further changes were made.

Pennsylvania set out its Article II as follows:

> That all men have a natural and unalienable right to worship Almighty God according to the dictates of their own consciences and understanding. And that no man ought or of right can be compelled to attend any religious worship, or erect or support any

> place of worship, or maintain any ministry, contrary to, or against, his own free will and consent.

Pennsylvania's Declaration of Rights continued: "Nor can any man, who acknowledges the being of a God, be justly deprived or abridged of any civil right as a citizen, on account of his religious sentiments or peculiar mode of religious worship." Vermont changed the words "who acknowledges the being of a God" to the much more restrictive and discriminating "who professes the protestant religion." In the beginning, then, there was no real religious freedom in Vermont. Fortunately this restriction was struck in the 1786 and 1793 versions, and today there is no religious qualification necessary to be protected in one's civil rights.

The last portion of the Pennsylvania declaration was completely changed. That declaration concluded as follows:

> And that no authority can or ought to be vested in, or assumed by any power whatever, that shall in any case interfere with, or in any manner control, the right of conscience in the free exercise of religious worship.

The Vermont Constitution of 1777 added the following: "nevertheless, every sect or denomination of people ought to observe the Sabbath, or the Lord's day, and keep up, and support, some sort of religious worship, which to them shall seem most agreeable to the revealed will of God."

The Vermont language remains intact except that the word "people" in the added sentence now reads "christian." We have no record of any reason for the change from "people" to "christian." We do know that the first Council of Censors proposed the change and the convention of 1786 adopted the proposed change. The word "christian." remains in the document to this day. The last section ("nevertheless, every sect . . . ought to observe the Sabbath") was added at Windsor.

Only two cases have been directly decided under this provision on the grounds of religion. In *Beauregard v. St. Albans* (1982) the lower court had held unconstitutional a provision in a codicil to a will. The will in question provided for the establishment of a board of trustees of five persons to manage and control an academy in Fairfax and one in St. Albans, Vermont. The codicil contained language making the acceptance of the trust contingent "that there shall be never more than one trustee . . . who shall belong to any one religious church or denomination at the same time."

The defendants raised two issues of constitutional concern: (1) whether the codicil violated the First and Fourteenth Amendments to the United States Constitution, and (2) whether the codicil violated Chapter 1, Article 3 of the Vermont Constitution.

The Vermont Supreme Court affirmed the lower court ruling in favor of the plaintiff. It stated that "the fact that the codicil's purpose is to maintain a separation of church and state and thus advance the values of the establishment clause does not save it." After reciting Chapter 1, Article 3, the court confirmed: "There is no question that the codicil's religious requirement 'interfere[s] with . . . the rights of conscience, in the free exercise of religious worship,' id., and is therefore unconstitutional. All that is required is a mere interference. In the present case the infringement is substantial; the plaintiff must either abandon his faith or convert in order to participate in the administration of his local school board."

In *State v. Chambers* (1984) the defendant was a member of a religious community. His daughter died at birth at a house he shared with other members of that religious community. The defendant attempted to obtain a death certificate, a prerequisite for burial, for his daughter. The chief medical examiner ruled that the cause of death could only be determined through an autopsy. Chambers refused to grant permission for the autopsy and buried the child without the requisite death certificate. He appealed his conviction for such action, claiming that Article 3 protected him because the conviction violated his right to the free exercise of his religion.

The court discussed first *Wisconsin v. Yoder* (1972), in particular, "the very concept of ordered liberty precludes allowing every person to make his (or her) own standards on matters of conduct in which society as a whole has important interests." The issue first must be whether the defendant's claim "is not merely a matter of personal preference, but one of deep religious conviction, shared by an organized group." The court affirmed the conviction, finding not that the church believes in burying the dead without autopsies but that the defendant's decision not to allow an autopsy was an individual one.

In *State v. De La Bruere* (1990) it appears that this article affords no greater protection of religious liberty than the First Amendment to the United States Constitution.

Article 4

Legal Remedy Secured to All

> Every person within this state ought to find a certain remedy, by having recourse to the laws, for all injuries or wrongs which he may receive in his person, property or character; he ought to obtain right and justice, freely, and without being obliged to purchase it; completely and without any denial; promptly and without delay; conformably to the laws.

Neither the Pennsylvania Declaration of Rights nor the Vermont Constitution of 1797 contains this Article 4. It was proposed by the first Council of Censors and incorporated into the Constitution of 1786, and remains in the present-day constitution unchanged.

This article guarantees the citizens of Vermont the right to a speedy resolution of any wrong done them. It also guarantees that no one will be denied access to the courts because of poverty. This latter guarantee seems to have been disregarded, as fees for filing and hearing and appealing have increased over the years. We have no cases defining "free" justice.

In *Levinsky v. Diamond* (1982) the plaintiff contended that this article gave substantive law protection to "character." The court held, however, that "the cited Vermont constitutional provision has never been held . . . to give rise to a substantive constitutional right. Instead, it has been treated as the Vermont equivalent of the federal Due Process Clause."

Historically in Vermont there had been no right of action on behalf of a wife against her husband, because under the common law they were one person and therefore could not sue each other. After the enactment of the first Rights of Married Woman Act in 1880, actions were permitted between husband and wife or wife and husband in certain instances. Yet, as late as 1934 in *Comstock v. Comstock,* a wife was not allowed to sue her husband for injuries caused to her by his gross negligence in operating a motor vehicle in which she was a guest.

However, *Greenwood v. Richard* (1973) specifically overruled *Comstock,* and a wife was permitted to bring an action in tort against her husband for injuries received from the negligent operation of an automobile by her husband. The court justified its ruling by noting that a woman is a "person" under Chapter 1, Article 4 of the state constitution. In so doing, the court rejected the doctrine that a husband and wife are one person.

A summons was issued after a hearing, ordering a Vermont resident, one Sally Ann Stoddard, to proceed to New Jersey, there to testify before a grand jury engaged in the investigation of a New Jersey criminal homicide. It was not claimed that Ms. Stoddard was any more than a material witness. She appealed the issuance of the summons. The Vermont Supreme Court held that the summons was a final judgment and thus appealable to the state's highest court. A refusal to permit the appeal would "clearly be contrary to Stoddard's guaranteed rights to a remedy at law" (*In re Stoddard,* 1983).

In the matter of prompt justice, it has been held that sentence reconsideration decisions do not come under this article (*State v. Dean,* 1987). In a claim for reversal because of appellate delay, the court held that this article would not be violated unless substantial prejudice resulted from the delay (*State v. Hall,* 1984).

Because of financial constraints, the supreme court temporarily delayed certain jury trials. Some attorneys challenged this delay, claiming a violation of this article (*In re Vermont Supreme Court Administrative Directive No.* 17, 1990). The court held that under Article 4 a temporary delay is not a denial of the right set out in this article.

Article 5

Internal Police

> That the people of this State by their legal representatives, have the sole, inherent, and exclusive right of governing and regulating the internal police of the same.

The 1777 Constitution adopted, as its Article 4, the third article of the Pennsylvania declaration verbatim. The 1786 Constitution added the words "by their legal representatives." Again we have no record of the reasons prompting the first Council of Censors to suggest adding that language. It is the article from which we derive the so-called police power of the state, which in effect is the power judged to be for the welfare of the state. It remains in the constitution as Article 5.

Slot machines had been made illegal by act of the legislature. In 1937 the legislature passed an act licensing such machines "when the result of their operation depended upon a substantial measure of skill on the part of the one then using the machine." In 1941 the possession of slot or pinball machines was again prohibited, and criminal penalties, including seizure of the machines, were imposed. The court held that the act of 1941 was constitutional as an exercise of the police power of the state. That power was defined in *Sowma v. Parker* (1941): "It is an attribute of sovereignty, or rather it is sovereignty itself." "It is given to the people of the State by our Constitution in Article V of Chapter 1 but apart from a written constitutional provision it is inherent in the states." "All property is held subject to general regulation by the Legislature under its police power for the common good and general welfare." "The power is so essential to the welfare of the people that it has been held to be impossible for a state to divest itself of its right and duty in respect of the full exercise thereof, and as well that the Federal Government cannot interfere in the exercise of that right and duty, except by virtue of some authority derived from the Constitution." "Subject to constitutional limitations, a state legislature is authorized to pass measures for the general welfare of the people of the state in the exercise of the police power, and is itself the judge of the necessity and expediency of the means adopted." "A proper exercise of the power is not a violation of the Fourteenth Amendment to the Federal Constitution even though property interests are affected. But the liberty guaranteed by the Amendment may not be interfered with, under the guise of protecting the public interest, by legislative action which is arbitrary or without reasonable relation to some purpose within the competency of the State to effect." "The test used to determine the constitutionality of the means employed by the Legislature is to inquire whether the restrictions it [police power] imposes on rights secured to individuals by the Bill of Rights are unreasonable and not whether it imposes any restrictions on such rights."

In *Bacon v. Boston & Maine R.R.* (1910) it was held that the railroads are subject to the police power; there it was said: "But each Legislature, unhampered by the acts of its predecessors, has and must have the right and duty to make such enactments for the well-being of the people as in a proper and strict sense are reserved to the people by virtue of the reservation of the police power."

In *Carty's Administrator v. Winooski* (1905) it was alleged that Winooski negligently maintained a lockup so that Carty, who had been locked up as a drunk, died through smoke inhalation. The court held that the village's power to maintain a lockup is an adjunct of the police power of the state guaranteed by Chapter 1, Article 5, and thus a governmental function. As municipalities are not liable for negligence in their governmental functions, the appeal was dismissed.

Commission action to preserve fish and wildlife has been held constitutional as a reasonable exercise of the police power (*Elliott v. Fish and Game Commission*, 1951).

In *Sabre v. Rutland R.R. Co.* (1913), a seminal case on police power, the court considered the constitutionality of the act of 1906 extending the jurisdiction of the Public Service Commission. Although the court divided three to two in upholding the act constitutional, all the justices recognized legislative authority to regulate railroads under the police power. The majority of the court characterized the police power in the following language: "The efficient exercise of the police power inherent in the people of this State is not to be frittered away by over-nice speculations upon the distribution of the powers of government. Our Constitution makes a general distribution of powers, but does not descend to those details which are found in some constitutions and which have resulted in discussions calculated to debilitate government itself."

The minority opinion was more concerned with the separation of powers and functions of the three departments of government. In both opinions will be found well reasoned and articulate discussions of the doctrine.

In *State v. Theriault* (1898) the authority of the state to regulate fish and game was upheld. The basis of the decision was the police power. Here the police power took precedence over Article 2 of Chapter 1 (taking property without payment) and Section 67 of Chapter 2 (rights to hunt and fish).

The regulation or prohibition of traffic in intoxicating liquor is likewise an exercise of the police power (*State v. Hodgson*, 1893). Yet in that case a limitation was suggested to such power. Certain constitutional rights, such as the right to trial by jury, cannot be abrogated in the name of police power.

Article 6

Officers as Servants of the People

> That all power being originally inherent in and co[n]sequently derived from the people, therefore, all officers of government, whether legislative or executive, are their trustees and servants; and at all times, in a legal way, accountable to them.

The 1777 Constitution adopted, as its Article 6, the language of Article IV of the Pennsylvania Declaration of Rights. The first Council of Censors felt it necessary to add the words "in a legal way." Again there is no reason for this change given in the report of that council. It is interesting that there is no specific language in the article making judges accountable.

In *Welch v. Seery* (1980) a resident of the town of Hartford asked the town clerk to disclose all fees accrued to the office of town clerk during the calendar years of 1976, 1977, and 1978. Upon being refused this information he brought an action for a declaratory judgment and injunctive relief against the town clerk personally. In dismissing the action the court said that "Article VI is but a truism of a republican form of government, and provides no private right of action. The remedy contemplated by it is that of popular election."

Article 7

Government for the People

> That government is, or ought to be, instituted for the common benefit, protection, and security of the people, nation, or community, and not for the particular emolument or advantage of any single man, family, or set of men, who are a part only of that community; and that the community hath an undubitable, unalienable, and indefeasible right, to reform or alter government, in such manner as shall be, by that community, judged most conducive to the public weal.

The 1777 Constitution adopted the comparable Pennsylvania article verbatim. Included in both articles were the words "or abolish" government.

The first Council of Censors submitted to the convention of 1786 a different version. The text as supplied by the council was not adopted by the convention. Instead the convention retained the 1777 version, dropping only "or abolish."

Vermont had always been a Sabbath observing state. Its Blue Laws contained provisions prohibiting businesses from operating on Sunday. Over the years, however, many exemptions had been approved by the legislature. Of course, Blue Laws are consistent with the theory that Sunday is a day of rest. An exemption had been created for stores with less than 5,000 square feet of interior customer selling space. Such stores contained in a 20,000 square foot enclosed shopping mall were not, however, exempted from the prohibition. It was a crime to violate this law and would subject the violator to a criminal penalty.

A criminal action was brought against the Ludlow Supermarkets. By agreement, the following question was certified to the Vermont Supreme Court:

> As applied to Ludlow Supermarkets, Inc., d/b/a Clark's Bennington IGA, a supermarket containing approximately 9,000 square feet of interior customer selling space that was open to the public on Sunday, May 17, 1981 and that was not exempted under 13 VSA Section 3355(a)(2) through (a)(7), does Title 13, Chapter 74 violate the United States or Vermont Constitutions?

After discussion of the equal protection law and its tests, the court directed its attention to Chapter 1, Article 7 of the Vermont Constitution. "The exemption at issue," said the court, "was expressly set out as to promote the economic health of small business enterprises." This being so, the obvious conclusion is that the legislature intended to benefit small "mom and pop" stores on Sunday. If the large stores were closed that day, the small stores would garner all Sunday business and prosper. This objective, however, runs into constitutional objections. The act was declared unconstitutional.

The police power can override other general restraints on state action if premised on an overriding public interest. Here the premise that small business enterprises "are essential and fundamental to the economy of the state" runs squarely into Article 7 when that article prohibits preferential legislation. Even the other stated purposes of the legislation are not protected by the police power. These aims were (1) the establishment of a common day of rest, and (2) energy conservation. The case was *State v. Ludlow Supermarkets, Inc.* (1982).

In *Vermont Woolen Corp. v. Wackerman* (1961) it was contended that a water classification scheme was intended to legislate for private purposes in violation of Article 7. The court disagreed, holding that the classifications did not give any water rights to particular individuals. They were merely descriptions of the standard of purity for the indicated uses.

The state may, however, make an appropriation in discharge of a moral obligation without violating Article 7. Otis Gross, acting as a deputy sheriff in the course of his duties, was murdered by a person under arrest and in his custody. The legislature appropriated $3,000 to his widow. Upon being presented with the request for the funds, the state auditor of accounts refused to comply. The widow brought a petition for a writ of mandamus to force the auditor to honor the appropriation. In *Gross v. Gates*, (1937), with one dissent, it was held that such an appropriation must be regarded as for a public purpose, and though a private person would receive the benefit, that would not constitute the act of appropriation a private one.

In *Town School District of Brattleboro v. School District No. 2 of Brattleboro* (1898) it was held, in effect, that municipal corporations are creatures of the legislature and may be treated differently without regard to Article 7. It has been held that Article 7 is akin to the equal protection clause of the Fourteenth Amendment to the United States Constitution. Under that reasoning a classification which is not arbitrary but has a reasonable connection with a permissible legislative or administrative purpose will be presumed constitutional (*Choquette v. Perrault*, 1989). In *Smith v. St. Johnsbury* (1988) the court said, in discussing Article 7, "It is clear from the text that this provision, like the equal protection clause of the Fourteenth Amendment to the United States Constitution, is aimed at equality between persons rather than between areas of the state."

The charter of the city of Burlington permitted the taxing of all nonresidential property not subject to other provisions at 120 percent of fair market value, while residential property was taxed at 100 percent of fair market value. The taxpayer claimed that the common benefit clause of Article 7 prohibits such discrimination. The court held in *In re Property of One Church Street* (1989) that "it surely will benefit some taxpayers more than others, but '[s]o long as the public purpose is paramount and the enactment reasonably related to that purpose, the statute is not made invalid thereby.'"

Veilleux v. Springer (1973) involved a statute under which, if a person pleaded not guilty to drunk driving, he would have his license suspended for six months, but if he pleaded guilty, he would not incur this civil penalty. This statute was held unconstitutional as violating Article 7. The court cited *United States v. Jackson*, 390 U.S. 570 at 583 (1968), where it was stated that a procedure need not be inherently coercive in order that it be held to impose an impermissible burden upon the assertion of a constitutional right. Here the act was held coercive in that it favored guilty pleas over not guilty pleas.

Vermont's Milk Control Act (1937), which regulated the price of milk, was challenged in *State v. Auclair* (1939) as being unconstitutional under Article 7 as violating due process and equal protection. During the Great Depression years the federal government and many states enacted milk control laws. In Vermont the general policy of the act was declared to be public health. The act also contained provisions for licensing sellers of milk.

Mr. Auclair sold without a license. Charged with violation of the act, he argued that the act, in particular the price-fixing provisions, violated Article 7. The court considered the principles contained in the act and determined that the finding by the legislature that public health was endangered was sufficient without further facts being brought forth.

Article 8

Free Elections; Rights of Freemen Therein

> That all elections ought to be free and without corruption, and that all freemen, having a sufficient, evident, common interest with, and attachment to the community, have a right to elect officers, and be elected into office, agreeably to the regulations made in this constitution.

This article in the Constitution of 1777 was taken verbatim from Article VII of the Pennsylvania Declaration of Rights. The Constitution of 1786 amended the article by adding the words "and without corruption." The article has not been amended since 1786.

The attorney general in an opinion has declared that the legislature may not restrict the rights to elect or be elected given by this article (Opinion of the Attorney General, 1958–60, 217).

In *Brownell v. Russell* (1904) the police chief of Burlington acted as chairman at a political party caucus. The rules of the police department prohibited such activity. Upon his claim of protection under Article 8 it was ruled that offices at a party caucus convention were not contemplated by the article.

Article 9

Citizens' Rights and Duties; Bearing Arms; Taxation

> That every member of society hath a right to be protected in the enjoyment of life, liberty, and property, and therefore is bound to contribute his proportion towards the expense of that protection, and yield his personal service, when necessary, or an equivalent thereto, but no part of any person's property can be justly taken from him, or applied to public uses, without his own consent, or that of the representative body of the freemen, nor can any man who is conscientiously scrupulous of bearing arms, be justly compelled thereto, if he will pay such equivalent; nor are the people bound by any law, but such as they have in like manner assented to, for their common good: and previous to any law being made to raise a tax, the purpose for which it is to be raised ought to appear evident to the Legislature to be of more service to the community than the money would be if not collected.

Here again Vermont, in its 1777 Constitution, adopted virtually verbatim the comparable article in the Pennsylvania Declaration of Rights. Yet the first Council of Censors added the words "or that of the representative body of the freemen," which were incorporated by the convention.

Although we are without any guide to the reasoning of the council or of the convention in including this phrase, it would appear that the inclusion granted to the legislature the complete power to tax.

This power to tax applies to all persons and property within the jurisdiction of the state and is limited only by federal supremacy (*Clark v. Burlington*, 1928). The *Clark* case also held that the constitutional requirement of proportional contributions did not restrict the state to methods of taxation that operated equally on all its inhabitants. When the classification conflicts with the federal or the state constitution, or with both, a court can declare it unconstitutional. As long as the legislature bases its classification on a rational ground, the presumption of constitutionality of a statute will be upheld.

The statutes will be most liberally construed to uphold the tax law if possible. However, in *In re Estate of Ruth Hart Eddy* (1977) a tax was held unconstitutional. There the court reiterated that the proportional contribution clause was the "practical equivalent" of the equal protection clause of the Fourteenth Amendment to the United States Constitution. It concluded that the tax in question violated the constitutions because there was no rational basis for the classifications in the act in question.

From these cases it is obvious that adoption by the state of the federal tax scheme would be upheld. In *Pabst v. Commissioner of Taxes* (1978) the court so decided. In *Pabst* the state gift tax was fixed as a percentage of the federal gift tax. The appellant Pabst based his constitutional arguments on the "piggyback" (i.e., percentage of the federal tax) feature of this law. In its opinion the court said that the legislature merely substituted the federal rate schedule for a separate Vermont rate schedule, and found nothing unconstitutional in such procedure. As the court indicated, the Vermont scheme was not unusual. Other state courts had approved such piggyback arrangements.

In *Leverson v. Conway* (1984) a taxpayer challenged a purchase and use tax. A taxpayer purchased a vehicle in Wisconsin and there paid a tax on the purchase. He then moved to Vermont. On attempting to register the vehicle, he was required to pay a 4 percent use tax on the low book value. He claimed that, as the car was a necessity, "strict scrutiny" should be the test of equal protection. The court held that the right to travel was not being infringed. Registration in Vermont was the key, said the court, and so "rational basis" was the test. The taxpayer's claim that the use tax violated the proportional contributions clause failed for the same reason. However, the U.S. Supreme Court vacated and remanded this case (1985). In *Alexander v. Barton* (1989) the court reiterated that the test for validity under Article 9 and its proportional contributions clause must be the rational basis test used for federal equal protection analysis.

In *Kruse v. Westford* (1985) the court held that the proportional contributions clause required that property be taxed at the same rate as other properties in a town. However, the court did not find that this standard had been violated in the case.

The village of Hardwick is located within the territorial limits of the town of Hardwick. The village constructed a hydroelectric plant in the town of Wolcott. A general exemption from taxation of property used for the public was limited by state statute, however, in cases of municipal electric light plants when located outside the town wherein the municipality owning the same is situated. The town of Wolcott taxed the real property of the hydroelectric plant located within its borders. The village contended, in *Village of Hardwick v. Town of Wolcott* (1925), that the law denies it equal protection under Article 9, Chapter 1 of the state constitution. Holding that the proportional contributions clause of the state constitution is, in effect, the equal protection clause in the federal constitution, the question is whether the statute violates the federal constitution. In that regard the court quoted *Bell's Gap Railroad v. Pennsylvania* (134 U.S. 232), where it stated: "The provisions in the Fourteenth Amendment that no state shall deny to any person within its jurisdiction the equal protection of the laws was not intended to prevent a state from adjusting its system of taxation in all proper and reasonable ways. We think that we are safe in saying that the Fourteenth Amendment was not intended to compel the State to adopt an iron rule of taxation." The test is, then, is the classification in the statute purely arbitrary? If so, the tax is unconstitutional. Here all municipal electric plants are treated equally, thus the tax was constitutional. See also *Stoneman v. Vergennes School District #5* (1980).

Inheritance taxes do not violate the proportional contributions clause because these taxes are not taxes on property but on the transmission of property. Transmission of property is not a natural right but a privilege accorded by the state. As the constitution protects property and not the transmission of property, the tax is not a violation of the constitution (*In re Hickoks Estate*, 1906).

It is necessary that the taxing authority have a clear standard of assessment. An act authorizing the city of Vergennes "to construct and repair sidewalks in the principal streets of the city" and permitting it to "assess the owners of the property through which or fronting which said sidewalks are constructed, so much of the expense thereof, as they shall deem just and equitable" was held to have too uncertain a standard. The court, in *Barnes v. Dyer* (1884), questioned the phrase "just and equitable." The opinion related that if the only interpretation of the phrase was just and equitable in view of the benefit to the premises fronting on the improved sidewalk, it would possibly be sufficient. If, however, the language is susceptible to numerous other interpretations, then the standard would not be clear: "Just and equitable in respect to what? The words import no special limitation." The act was held unconstitutional.

The taxing power of the state in Article 9 is restricted to public uses. The Vermont Home Mortgage Credit Agency was authorized to issue negotiable notes and bonds to provide resources for the purchase of mortgage obligations. The act creating the agency set out findings that the agency would benefit the people of Vermont in their "health, safety, welfare and prosperity, and is a public purpose, and that the agency will be performing an essential governmental function. It is specifically found and determined that this Act is necessary to assure an adequate supply of capital . . . for the state's growing population."

The act was challenged as being for a private rather than a public purpose (*Vermont Home Mortgage Credit Agency v. Montpelier National Bank*, 1970). If the act would affect low-income families with incidental benefits to middle-income families, the defendant declared it would not challenge the act. An incidental benefit to the public is proper. But, argued the bank, when an undeserving class is benefitted as a main part of the legislation, then it is for a private use. As the purpose of the act was not related specifically to low-income needs and slum clearance projects, the purpose became private rather than public.

The court, in deciding the issue, likened the act to one passed in 1867 that authorized towns in southern Vermont to aid in the construction of railroads. There the court said that aid authorized will almost certainly benefit private corporations or individuals, "but if a general public benefit is accomplished, the money appropriated is made of 'more service to the community than it would be if not collected.'"

A court must accept the statement of purpose of the legislature as true. A public purpose within the purview of Article 9 "is a question for the Legislature to decide, and concerning which it has large discretion, which the courts can control only, if at all, in very exceptional cases" (*Burlington v. Central Vermont Railway Co.,* 1908). Insofar as the legislative declarations and findings are subject to judicial review, they are determinative unless it can clearly be seen that a law purporting to protect the public welfare bears no rational relation to that purpose.

Education has been declared by the court to be a public purpose (*Vermont Educational Buildings Financing Agency v. Mann,* 1968).

The ability of the legislature to authorize exemptions from taxation has been litigated in three cases. In *Colton & More v. Montpelier* (1899) the court held that the state had the power to tax under Article 9 and that that power included the power to exempt. As the legislature can delegate taxing powers to the municipalities, it must be granted, as is the state, the power to exempt from taxation.

In re Hickok's Estate (1906) established the power to exempt "charitable, educational or religious societies or institutions."*Governor Clinton Council Inc. v. Koslowski* (1979) determined that the legislature may exempt specific organizations from property taxes in a town without the consent of the town. There the legislature exempted boy scout organizations from property taxes. The town of Stratton had attempted to tax property of the body scouts located in its territory. The court held the exemption valid.

"Double taxation is frowned upon," said the court in *Poulin v. Danville* (1969). In that case two towns claimed that Poulin's property was located within their borders. Both towns could not tax the property, and the towns had to bear the burden of determining where the property was located. Poulin had based his contention on Article 9. Although frowned upon, double taxation is not per se unconstitutional (*Burlington Electric Dept. v. Vermont Dept. of Taxes,* 1990).

Property must be appraised for tax at its fair market value. But Article 9 mandates that the values must be uniform, and for that reason it is necessary that all comparable properties to the instant property be considered. In *Heindel v. Grafton* (1981) the taxpayer's property, after appeal, was appraised at $35,900.

Three years later it was reappraised at $44,050, which was reduced to $43,900. On appeal the court held that the reassessment was proper if it resulted in a uniform rate.

A more egregious case was decided in 1973. In *Bookstaver v. Westminster*, comparable properties were listed at $44,120, $21,380, and $24,940, with the taxpayer's property listed at $70,099. Here the case was reversed with instructions to find the correct appraisal based on a fair market value but uniform with comparable properties.

A deputy sheriff was killed while serving a civil writ. The legislature awarded $3,000 to his widow. The auditor of accounts refused to issue a warrant for this amount to the widow, claiming that the award was for a private use. While agreeing that the award was to a private person, the court nevertheless distinguished between a gift and the discharge of a moral obligation without violating Article 9, even though a private person receives the benefit (*Gross v. Gates*, 1937).

Article 10

Rights of Persons Accused of Crime; Personal Liberty; Waiver of Jury Trial

> That in all prosecutions for criminal offenses, a person hath a right to be heard by himself and his counsel; to demand the cause and nature of his accusation; to be confronted with the witnesses; to call for evidence in his favor, and a speedy public trial by an impartial jury of the country; without the unanimous consent of which jury, he cannot be found guilty; nor can he be compelled to give evidence against himself; nor can any person be justly deprived of his liberty, except by the laws of the land, or the judgment of his peers; provided, nevertheless, in criminal prosecutions for offenses not punishable by death, the accused, with the consent of the prosecuting officer entered of record, may in open court or by a writing signed by him and filed with the court, waive his right to a jury trial and submit the issue of his guilt to the determination and judgment of the court without a jury.

The Vermont Constitution of 1777 incorporated Article IX of the Pennsylvania Bill of Rights but added the word "public" after the word "speedy," making the trial speedy and public. The original Pennsylvania and Vermont articles ended with the words "judgment of his peers." In 1924 by Article of Amendment 38 the balance of Article 10 was added. In that amendment offenses not punishable "by imprisonment in the state prison" were included. This language was eliminated by Article of Amendment 46, adopted in 1974.

A history of the abuses that Article 10 was designed to eliminate is found in *State v. Conlin* (1855). This article defines many of the rights of the accused in criminal cases. It is derived from the common law of England, which remains in effect unless changed by statute. In *State v. Prouty* (1920) the defendant Prouty was charged with a misdemeanor but was not arraigned, nor did he plead before the jury was drawn. After the jury was drawn but before trial he waived the reading of the information (charge) and pleaded not guilty. The court held that such a waiver cured any defect, particularly in the case of a misdemeanor. The court further stated that it was the purpose of an arraignment to identify the respondent (defendant), acquaint him with the accusation, and take his plea. In making motions, in addressing the jury, and in waiving his rights, there was no doubt that the defendant was identified, knew of the charges against him, and, by contesting through the jury selection process, had pleaded not guilty. The court concluded that the law should never elevate form over substance.

In Vermont crimes are classified as felonies or misdemeanors. Felonies are of a more serious nature. The article does not differentiate between felonies and misdemeanors:

> The provisions of the Vermont Constitution in 1793 and the course of legislation in this state before and since that time, leave no doubt that the people have regarded all criminal causes as proper for cognizance of a jury. It is our belief that the framers of the Vermont Constitution intended to secure to an accused, in prosecutions for all "criminal offenses," the right to trial by jury (*State v. Becker*, 1972).

The right of trial by a jury of twelve men was first decided in Vermont in the case of *In re Powers* (1853). Powers was found intoxicated and placed in jail by the sheriff of Windsor County. Upon becoming sober, he was questioned as to where he obtained the liquor. The magistrate interrogating the prisoner was not satisfied with the answers and refused to release Mr. Powers. The court held that an inquiry was being held and not a trial, and therefore no jury was required.

The requirement of trial by jury only means that the final judgment must be by a trial by jury. In *State v. Peterson* (1869) the defendant was tried before a recorder in court without a jury and was convicted. His attempt to appeal to the county court was denied because the crime of which he had been convicted permitted the recorder to make a final judgment without appeal. The Vermont Supreme Court reversed, holding that the act violated the respondent's right to trial by jury. The court further, by dicta, indicated that if an appeal had been allowed to a court where the defendant could have been tried by a jury of twelve, the act would have been sustained.

JURY TRIAL

The Constitution of Pennsylvania, on which Vermont modeled its constitution, used the term "country" as the place where jury trials could be held. Vermont adopted that term. Although Pennsylvania amended its constitution to substitute "vicinage" for "country," Vermont never followed suit and remains the only state where the trial must be by a jury of the "country."

The interpretation to be given to that term was discussed in *State v. Brown* (1931). In that case, property stolen in Washington County was received by Mr. Brown in Chittenden County. Under the statute then pertaining, prosecution of a receiver was permitted in the county in which the goods were stolen. Brown claimed that this violated Article 10.

Justice Slack, in writing the opinion, set out the history of the jury process. Criminal offenses were generally deemed to be local and subject to prosecution only in the county in which they were committed. Thus at common law a person had a right to be tried by a jury of his neighborhood or county. If the common law rule is law in Vermont, then the statute would be unconstitutional. The discussion, however, concerned the reason for the word "country" and the breadth to be given to that word. The court was satisfied that Vermont's constitution was framed to enlarge the scope of the legislative authority over the venue of trials of criminal cases.

The interpretation of the jury venue set out in the *Brown* case was confirmed in *State v. Murphy* (1976). Vermont's district courts are set in units which may contain more than one county. Murphy allegedly committed rape on an eleven-year-old girl in Caledonia County. Both the district court and county court used the same courtroom facilities in Caledonia County. Because of scheduling conflicts, the district judge moved the trial of the case to Essex County, a county contained within the same unit, 4, as Caledonia County. The judge drew a jury from the jury list comprised of citizens of Essex County.

The defendant asked that the prosecution be dismissed because of improper jury selection. He claimed that the list should have contained names from the three counties comprising Unit 4. The court cited *Brown* as precedent that the word "country" permitted a change of venue if the legislature so permitted.

Juveniles have always obtained better treatment than adults under Article 10. Three juveniles, residents of a group home, were suspected of breaking into two condominiums across the highway from the home. The juveniles were interrogated separately by the state police. E.T.C. was, according to the troopers, advised of his *Miranda* rights, acknowledged that he understood them, and agreed to talk. While E.T.C. was being interrogated, the director of the group home was present, and although he never consulted with the juvenile prior to the interrogation, he did advise the juvenile to cooperate with the police and indicated that "things would go easier if he did." The juvenile made statements inculpating himself in the breaking and entering.

E.T.C. moved to suppress the statements he made. Upon a ruling denying his motion, an appeal was taken to the Vermont Supreme Court. The court held that a juvenile was entitled to assistance prior to an appearance in court, and the same right accrued to him before interrogation. The justices set out three criteria for a juvenile to voluntarily waive his right against self-incrimination: (1) opportunity to consult with an adult (2) who must be genuinely interested in the welfare of the juvenile and is completely independent from the prosecution and

(3) who must be informed and be aware of the rights guaranteed to the juvenile (*In re E.T.C.*, 1982; see pp. 59–60).

That part of Article 10 which reads "that in all prosecutions for criminal offenses, a person hath a right to be heard by himself and his counsel" was discussed in *In re Southard* (1966). Southard was charged with breaking and entering and assigned counsel by the court because he was indigent. He pled guilty, then not guilty by reason of insanity, and finally pled guilty in court through his attorney, although personally remaining silent. At common law it was required that an accused had to enter all pleas personally. The Vermont Supreme Court held that under Article 10 the defendant need not personally make a plea.

The court in *State v. Saari* (1989) discussed the right of a defendant to allocution (which gives defendants the opportunity to address the bench prior to sentencing). It was contended that statutory minimum sentences violated the defendant's right to allocution. The court declared that allocution was a tradition of the common law and not a constitutional right. The court further said that the legislature could even eliminate the tradition if it wished.

RIGHT OF COUNSEL

Vermont follows the federal rule (*United States v. Wade*, 1967) relative to criminal proceedings (*State v. Howe*, 1978), the right to counsel attaching at a critical stage of criminal proceedings. When the critical stage has arrived is, of course, a question of fact. The court held that the actual taking of physical evidence which is nontestimonial is not a critical stage of the criminal proceedings (*Howe*). Nor is the taking of a blood sample, being nontestimonial, a critical stage (*State v. Kennison*, 1987).

In re Moses (1960) held that the rules relating to the right to counsel were the same for minors as for adults. In that case a minor pled guilty to a crime. He had been advised that he could have counsel at the expense of the state. He was also advised that he could plead guilty without either a guardian *ad litem* (who was not appointed) or an attorney. The court held that as long as the minor could intelligently plead, he did not need either an attorney or a guardian *ad litem*. There had been no violation of Article 10.

The legislature shortly thereafter enacted a statute guaranteeing counsel for a minor charged with a felony. The statute required a guardian *ad litem* when no counsel was representing the minor. In *In re Mears* (1964) a felony conviction of a minor was overturned when it appeared that although a guardian *ad litem* had been appointed, no attorney had been appointed. The court held, however, that no counsel was needed for the minor, when, with a guardian *ad litem*, a plea of guilty was entered in a misdemeanor case involving Mr. Mears.

Later, in *In re Dobson* (1965), the court held that a guardian *ad litem* was always to be appointed whenever a minor was charged with a crime. In that case a lawyer had been assigned to represent the defendant, a minor. No guardian *ad litem*, however, was appointed. The court overruled only that portion of *Moses* that did not require the appointment of a guardian *ad litem*. The court further held that a lawyer could not be both an attorney and guardian *ad litem* at the same time. To permit such would have the attorney represent his client and also be the client. It would be better to separate the two roles.

The right to counsel means the right to be represented by competent counsel who must render effective assistance. The counsel appointed or retained must have sufficient ability and experience to represent a defendant fairly, to present his defense, and to protect his rights. Along with this is the presumption that a member of the bar is competent.

In *State v. Rushford* (1968) the defendant was arraigned on October 12, 1963, charged with forging checks. He asked for time to obtain counsel. The court appointed an experienced attorney to represent the defendant. On March 17, 1964, after repeated conferences with the attorney, the defendant personally entered a plea of guilty to the several counts. The court found that the assigned counsel had the experience and knowledge to render effective assistance of counsel to the defendant.

In a later case, *In re Kasper* (1982), the court established that the standard was "that of 'reasonable competence' as measured by the prevailing standards in the conduct of the defendant's case." The court proceeded to deny postconviction relief requested on the grounds of ineffective assistance of counsel. *In re Bruyette* (1988) confirmed the standards set out in *Kasper*.

Although the state is required to furnish counsel, it is only required to furnish counsel to the indigent. In *State v. Gomez* (1915) the defendant was represented by counsel paid for by himself. During and after the trial he asked that his counsel be reimbursed by the state, claiming that Article 10 mandated the state to pay for counsel whenever one would be assigned. The court held that only indigents were entitled to free counsel and that the trial court had discretion to make the determination of indigency.

Although counsel is required, it has been held that this is a personal right and may be waived (*State v. Bliss*, 1975). The knowing and intelligent waiver of the right to counsel depends on the facts and circumstances surrounding the case, including the background, experience, and conduct of the accused (*State v. Hartman*, 1975). He must also be aware of the nature of the charges and the range of the allowable punishment at the time of the waiver. In *Hartman* the case was reversed because of these insufficiencies. Nor will silence constitute a waiver (*In re Huard*, 1965). However, a determination by the trial court that counsel has been waived competently and intelligently will stand unless it is demonstrated that the waiver was so unjustified as to amount to a deprivation of the respondent's constitutional rights.

CAUSE AND NATURE OF ACCUSATION

Article 10 further declares that "a person hath a right to demand the cause and nature of his accusation." The Vermont Supreme Court has held that the word "demand" does not place the burden of requesting information on the defendant but means that the information must be found in the criminal complaint. This enables the defendent to plead intelligently to the accusation. Nothing extraneous to the complaint may make the complaint sufficient. All that is required is a reasonable certainty of the crime charged (see *State v. Villa,* 1918). A criminal complaint satisfies Article 10 if it sufficiently states the nature of the offense charged when it sets forth with such particularity as will reasonably indicate the exact offense, and will enable the accused to make intelligent preparation for his defense. It must be sufficiently clear so that he may plead double jeopardy in a subsequent prosecution for the same offense. It must also allege an essential fact affecting the degree of punishment (*State v. Bradley,* 1985).

Villa also held that the legislature could not legalize a form of criminal complaint that failed to meet the requirements of Article 10. Earlier the court had confronted this question in *State v. Comstock* (1854) and held that the legislature may prescribe the form of indictment or information provided no constitutional provision is violated.

The necessity for particularity in a complaint does not, apparently, apply to "minor" crimes. In *State v. Conlin* (1855) and *State v. Comstock* (1854) defendants were prosecuted in a justice of the peace court, a minor court, not a court of record, for the crime of selling intoxicating liquor. The record of the justice in *Conlin* showed that one arrested for intoxication testified that he bought the liquor from Conlin. The justice of the peace issued a warrant for Conlin's arrest "to answer the matters alleged against him in the foregoing testimony." The court held that Article 10 has reference to that class of criminal cases denominated "high crimes," the punishment of which affects life, liberty, and reputation, and exposes the offender to infamous corporal suffering; and has no application to those minor offenses that clearly concern the regulation of the internal police of the state. The court further held that in cases of minor offenses punishable by fine only or imprisonment in the county jail for a limited time, the legislature may constitutionally provide for trial upon informal or merely oral complaints.

In *State v. Woodmansee* (1964) the state, during the fifth day of a six-day trial, was permitted to amend a count in larceny to a count in arson. The court reversed and ordered a new trial on the amended count. The court said:

> Certainly here the objection is technical. Taking original counts three and four together, the respondent can hardly have failed reasonably to have apprehended the nature of the offenses with which he was charged. But, technical or not, this is an area of constitutional sensitivity. The form of the charge is the responsibility of the prosecuting authority. It is not unjust to hold that authority strictly accountable for substantive shortcomings in its pleadings.

> To transmute the text to a subjective issue of the respondent's understanding of a defective charge would place the constitutional purpose in danger. Authoritarian caprice, against which the whole structure of constitutional law was erected as a barrier, could begin again to outflank our objectives of justice and fair dealing. Since the substantive change in count three was made after five days of trial, during which time the principal part of the State's case was put in evidence, allowance of that amendment ought to have been conditioned on a new trial on that count. We must, therefore, impose that condition here.

The court in *State v. Christman* (1977) did permit an amendment that did not charge a new and different offense.

The court reversed a conviction for speeding when the information was a form with boxes stating several specific criminal offenses involving the operation of motor vehicles, with an "x" in the box for speeding, holding that such a form lacked the particularity demanded by Article 10. (*State v. Chapman,* 1966). It also reversed a conviction for harassment by telephone where the statute listed certain prohibited acts and the charge included all the prohibited acts strictly in the language of the statute. No specific act having been alleged, the court reversed on grounds of lack of specificity (*State v. Hastings,* 1974).

The court has been particularly careful when disjunctive language is used in the statute and in the complaints. In *State v. Rouillard* (1935) the complaint was in the disjunctive. It alleged that the defendant "did. . .employ or *cause to be employed* certain means, to wit: by inserting or *causing to be inserted* a certain instrument or instruments." After trial and while the jury was deliberating, the prosecution was granted permission to strike the underlined words. It was held too late. Amendments of substance must be made before trial (*State v. Rouillard,* 1935). The use of the word "or" is not necessarily fatal. Where the words used, for example, "forged or counterfeit," mean the same thing, the statement of the offense would not be uncertain (*State v. Woodmansee,* 1970).

It is sufficient to charge a statutory offense in the words of the act if every fact necessary to constitute the offense is charged or is necessarily implied by following the language. However, if the *manner* in which the act is done makes it criminal, the manner becomes a constituent part of the offense and must be set forth (*State v. Persons,* 1946).

CONFRONTATION OF WITNESSES

Citing *Smith v. Illinois* (1968) the Vermont Supreme Court has held that the right to confront witnesses is not only constitutional but is a "fundamental" right which would bind Vermont without a constitutional provision (*State v. Berard,* 1974). As the right is a common law right it is subject to the common law exceptions and limitations.

In a footnote (2) in the case of *State v. Sprague* (1984) the court held that the Vermont confrontation clause provided the same right as the confrontation clause of the Sixth Amendment to the United States Constitution. Nor does it have a greater scope than the Sixth Amendment (*State v. Roberts*, 1990). The right is a trial right, that is, it pertains only to how a trial is conducted, is a fundamental requirement for a fair trial, and is specifically related to criminal prosecutions (*State v. Morse*, 1967). It guarantees that a witness will be cross-examined so that his recollection will be tested as well as compelling the witness to face the jury so that they may observe him and judge whether he is worthy of belief. It was also held in *State v. French* (1989) that "the threshold question in examining a confrontation clause claim is whether the defendant 'was prohibited from engaging in otherwise appropriate cross-examination.'" This rule is subject to exceptions. One exception is when a witness is unavailable but has given testimony at a prior proceeding.

In *State v. Sprague* (1984) a deposition was admitted into evidence as long as the circumstances under which it was given closely approximated those that surround a typical trial. In that case the declarant had testified under oath, the defendant was there represented by counsel who had had an opportunity to cross-examine the declarant, and the proceedings were recorded and were conducted before a judicial tribunal.

In order to guarantee the right of confrontation it would seem necessary to compel the attendance of witnesses. This is true, but such witnesses must be shown to be able to offer competent and material evidence (*State v. Kelly*, 1973). Thus a court is not required to issue compulsory process for anyone the accused may designate as a witness. The burden is on the defendant to show the materiality of such evidence. Failure to carry the burden justifies the court in refusing to issue compulsory process (*State v. Dragon*, 1972).

■ EVIDENCE

In *State v. Goshea* (1979) the defendant was accused of killing one Rodgers and then burning the body. His defense was that Rodgers had in fact killed a "look-alike" and then disappeared to avoid prosecution for a felony. The evidence proving the body of Rodgers was conflicting. During the trial the prosecutor received a telephone call from a person, found later to be a substantial citizen, who stated that he saw a person in Burlington who strongly resembled Rodgers. The prosecutor continued the trial without disclosing this telephone call to the defendant. In summing up to the jury the prosecutor argued: "I submit to you, ladies and gentlemen, that it is ridiculous. . . . [After committing the crime, Rodgers] would have had to vanish. *He would have had to leave the State of Vermont somehow, having been seen by no one and never be seen again.*" The defendant discovered this evidence after he had been found guilty of first-degree murder and sentenced to life imprisonment.

The trial court denied a motion for a new trial. On appeal it was held that the defendant's right to a fair trial had been violated. Evidence favorable to the defendant and known by the prosecutor must be divulged to the defendant. Suppressing the evidence and then stressing its nonexistence deprived the defendant of the fair trial guaranteed by Article 10. The conviction was reversed and the case was remanded for a new trial.

In *State v. Johnson* (1983), a prosecution for driving while intoxicated, defendant attempted to put in evidence the fact that he had voluntarily taken a breath test. He claimed the right to introduce the evidence under that provision of Article 10 that says a person has a right to call for evidence in his favor. The court held, however, that "the 'evidence in his favor' must be otherwise admissible under the law of evidence; the Constitution does not guarantee the admission of unduly prejudicial or misleading evidence." The conviction was affirmed. The evidence must conform to the law of evidence (*State v. Potter*, 1987). Nor does the Constitution require the admission of misleading or unduly prejudicial evidence (*State v. Larose*, 1988).

SPEEDY TRIAL

Courts must treat each case on its own facts. In *State v. Mahoney* (1965) the court discussed the speedy trial provisions of Article 10 during its discussion of the contentions of the defendant. The court posed the following question: Did the delay between arrest and trial deprive the defendant of a speedy trial as guaranteed by Article 10 of Chapter 1 of the Vermont Constitution? The court concluded that the right to a speedy trial serves three purposes. First, if the accused is confined prior to trial, it protects him against long imprisonment prior to a determination of guilt or innocence. Second, it protects the defendant against "prolonged anxiety and public embarrassment" which follows an untried accusation of crime. Third, it protects the accused from delay which might deprive him of witnesses or dull their memories.

The defendant can waive this right. In *State v. Mahoney* the court reviewed the record and noted that the delays were either requested by defendant or came about through a request for change of counsel. The court concluded that on all the facts and circumstances the defendant had effectively waived a right to an "earlier trial."

In *State v. Dragon* (1972) the court was faced with a delay of seven and one-half months from date of arrest to date of trial. During that period, the defendant was confined in state prison on an unrelated conviction. The defendant claimed that he had been denied his constitutional right to a speedy trial. The court pointed out that the right to a speedy trial is generally different from other constitutional rights because delay can work to the advantage of either the accused or the prosecution. Although the burden is on the prosecutor and the court to bring cases to trial speedily, nevertheless the defendant has the burden of claiming this right reasonably.

A balancing test weighs the conduct of both the prosecution and the defendant. Four factors must be taken into consideration:

1. Length of delay
2. The reason for the delay
3. The defendant's assertion of his right
4. Prejudice to the defendant

Here the court held that the delay was not a denial of the right to a speedy trial. They did not hold that such a delay would be a denial under other circumstances. The four factors were stated in *State v. Recor* (1988).

As part of its procedural authority, the Vermont Supreme Court issued their Administrative Order No. 5. That order requires a trial to be held within six months from the date of arrest. If the state is not prepared to proceed at that time the case may be dismissed unless the state receives an extension based on good cause. In *State v. Snide* (1984) the defendant argued that his case, which had been dismissed without prejudice, should have been dismissed with prejudice, as Administrative Order No. 5 had been violated. The court held that the order was part of the internal operating procedures and neither grants nor deprives a defendant of any constitutional right. A speedy trial violation is not predetermined by its operation. Such a right cannot be quantified into a specified number of days or months.

Prejudice to the defendant is the most important factor in analyzing speedy trial issues. In *State v. Franklin* (1978) the court held that a delay of eighteen months from citation to trial, not brought about by defendant, was prejudicial as a matter of law and reversed the conviction. Thirteen months of the delay was due to the judge's failure to act on a motion. Because of this fault being on the court, the matter should have been dismissed as soon as the motion to dismiss on grounds of denial of speedy trial was made.

The prejudice must be to the defense at trial. The defendant's personal embarrassment is not per se prejudicial (*State v. Recor*, 1988). Where there has been alleged appellate delay, the defendant must show substantial prejudice (*State v. Hall*, 1984).

JURY TRIAL

It has been held since the case of *Lincoln v. Smith* (1855) that a jury trial must be granted in any criminal case and that the jury must be of twelve persons. In that case a trial was held in a minor court that allowed a six-person jury or trial by judge. An appeal was allowed to the court with a twelve-person jury, "and it is quite well settled, that if a legislature pass an act giving to a justice of the peace power to hear and decide a cause, without the intervention of a jury but the act gives a right of appeal to a court which tries causes by a jury, it is no such violation of the right of trial by jury, as to render the act unconstitutional; although had the judgment of the justice been final, it might have been."

Citing *Lincoln v. Smith* on that point, the court in *State v. Peterson* (1869) held unconstitutional an act granting finality to the decision of a justice of the peace court, where no jury of twelve persons was allowed, nor was an appeal to a higher court which would have convened a twelve-person jury permitted.

In *In re Kennedy* (1883) the court held that such appeal cannot be conditioned on defendant's giving bail. The statute under consideration permitted an appeal to a county court. There bail may be imposed but not as a condition of an appeal. That the jury is to be the common law jury of twelve is unequivocably stated in *State v. Hirsch* (1917).

A jury is an integral element of a court in its search for justice. Its verdict must follow the charge of the court solely on admissible legal evidence and be free from the taint of extraneous considerations and influences. The test is not whether irregular matters actually influenced the result, but whether they have the capacity to do so.

In *State v. Ovitt* (1967) defendant was convicted of rape and assault to commit rape. On appeal he alleged prejudicial error in portions of the general charge and of the additional instructions given to the jurors at the opening of the term of court. The Vermont Supreme Court held that the "initial charge to the general panel of jurors was erroneous, and even as supplemented left much to be desired." The instructions in question contained the following language: "you may not be aware of it but, at this time you are about to participate in what is known as the law enforcement functions of the County of Essex. . . . and it will be a rewarding experience to you as your part in law enforcement in this County." The trial court attempted a clarification, which did not clarify. The defendant asked for a dismissal; the trial court denied the motion. In the charge to the jury at the conclusion of the trial a further attempt was made to clarify their functions. The appellate court held that with all the attempts at clarification, the jury might still be confused and misled as to its function. Additionally, the court officers purchased liquor at the meals furnished to the jury. No liquor was furnished during their deliberations. In this regard the court held that it was better not to furnish liquor to a jury during trial, but with no prejudice shown that alone would not cause a reversal. The cumulative effect of all the errors, however, caused a reversal and a remand for a new trial.

A statement by a judge to a news reporter that "a plea of guilty shows that the defendant has some kind of repentance for what he did would not hold true in a trial. In that case he would not be dealt with as leniently" led to his being disciplined. The court cited *Ovitt* and concluded that "any pronouncement relative to the right to trial by jury as made by this judge may have a chilling effect on that constitutionally protected right."

It is fundamental that a defendant in a criminal trial has a constitutional right to a trial by an impartial jury. In *State v. Holden* (1978) that question of an impartial jury was raised on appeal following a conviction against the defendant. When the jury was being examined on voir dire before trial, one juror on three separate occasions stated her belief that a defendant had an obligation to prove his innocence. Although the state attempted to rehabilitate the juror, the court found that she should have been dismissed as being unfit to follow the presumption of innocence. "If upon examination a juror shows a state of mind evincing a fixed opinion, bias or prejudice, she is properly subject to challenge for cause." "If a prospective juror has a belief that a defendant carries any burden whatsoever of proving his innocence, that juror is removable for cause." The defendant used his last peremptory challenge to remove the juror from the panel. The court held that where the record disclosed that the defendant had one more juror he wished to challenge peremptorily, the case must be reversed. The court distinguished the fact that all peremptory challenges had been used from *Lattrell v. Swain* (1968), where all the peremptory challenges had not been exhausted.

The court further refined the peremptory challenge dilemma in *State v. White* (1982). In that case, the trial court was found in error for not dismissing a juror for cause, but not reversible error, as no prejudice was shown. Here, as in *Holden*, all peremptory challenges were exercised, but the defendant failed to indicate that there was anyone on the panel, as eventually constituted, that he desired to remove. This failure to show prejudice required affirmance of the judgment against defendant.

The right to an impartial jury can be violated when any improper suggestions are made by the court.

> The Constitution of Vermont, Chapter 1, Article 10, gives anyone charged with a violation of the law a right to be heard by himself and counsel. An indication from the presiding judge, to whom a jury looks for guidance, that he belittles, or looks with disfavor upon the conduct of counsel could well be reflected in the consideration by the jury of the rights of the respondent whom the counsel represents (*State v. Hedding*, 1961).

A minor brought before a juvenile court is not, however, entitled to a jury trial. Casimiro Gomez, a minor, was brought before a municipal court sitting as a juvenile court. He claimed that as he was charged with the commission of a crime, he was entitled to a jury trial. The juvenile court statute did not permit a jury trial. The juvenile court judge denied the request. The supreme court affirmed, holding that juvenile proceedings were not penal but protective. The child was not to be punished. "It steps in merely to save the child from the evil tendencies of its situation, and to give it more care and training, to the end that it may become a more worthy and useful member of society" (*In re Gomez, 1943*).

In Vermont in the trial of a felony a jury must be sequestered, and when the jury is permitted to be released from the custody of the court there must be consent by the defendant. In *State v. Bailey* (1984) the defendant was charged with a felony. His attorney filed a waiver of jury sequestration. The defendant did not sign the document. He claimed on appeal that the waiver is personal to him, and then only after the court had explained such right to him. It had previously been held that the defendant's right to an unbiased jury was a personal right and may be waived only by the defendant personally. In *Bailey* the court further refined the rule by declaring that only when bias had been shown during the trial did the right become personal. Without prejudice being shown, the issue became whether counsel had authority to waive jury sequestration on behalf of defendant without his knowledge before trial and in the absence of any suggestion of bias on the record. The *Bailey* court followed the general rule that trial counsel controls the procedural aspects of a case. It follows, then, that a tactical or procedural waiver executed by an attorney on behalf of his client is binding. The conviction was affirmed.

A waiver of a jury trial stands on a different footing. Here Article 10 specifically says:

> The accused, with the consent of the prosecuting officer entered of record, may in open court or by a writing signed by him and filed with the court, waive his right to a jury trial and submit the issue of his guilt to the determination and judgment of the court without a jury.

In *State v. Ibey* (1976) the defendant's attorney filed a motion for trial by court, signed only by him and not Ibey. The court reversed the conviction, stating that "the failure to fulfill the constitutional requirements as to the defendant's waiver requires reversal."

A defendant who waives his right to a trial by jury under a misapprehension not engendered by himself may have his conviction reversed. Defendant in *State v. Bliss* (1975) was charged with a misdemeanor such that no assignment of a public defender was authorized. He claimed, however, that he was given to understand that he could only have a trial by jury if he obtained counsel. The court, in dicta, declared that "to attempt to make him believe that the right to trial by jury is conditioned on his being represented by counsel may render any waiver, even those in proper and constitutional form, involuntary, and is not to be condoned."

Civil hearings do not demand a jury trial. A refusal to submit to an alcohol test is a summary hearing of a civil nature and thus does not require a jury trial (*Shaw v. Vermont District Court*, 1989). Nor does the determination of legal issues require a jury (*State v. Ryea*, 1990).

SELF-INCRIMINATION

Article 10 declares that no person can be compelled to give evidence against himself. There need be no self-incrimination. *State v. Duncan* (1906) was a conspiracy case against ten persons. Five of the ten had given incriminating evidence before a grand jury, which became the basis of the indictment. They all claimed that their privilege against self-incrimination had been violated because they had not been advised of their right to refuse to testify.

The court declared that the common law immunity guaranteed by Article 10 of the Vermont Constitution is an option of refusal and not a prohibition of inquiry. The privilege against self-incrimination is a personal one. It may be waived if it is not seasonably asserted. If a defendant testifies without objection, he will be deemed to have testified voluntarily and waived his right. The defendant is not protected because he was not notified of the privilege and warned of the possible consequences of giving incriminating testimony. The court did state that such notice and warning are usually given. In *In re Mackenzie* (1927), *State v. Duncan* is quoted approvingly.

During the days of Prohibition under the Eighteenth Amendment to the United States Constitution, many states passed acts designed to ferret out sellers or purveyors of intoxicating liquor. A Vermont statute adopted in 1921 required each person convicted of intoxication to disclose the name of the party from whom the liquor was obtained. The court has held that Article 10 "embodies a safeguard of civil liberty as sacred and inviolable as any of the fundamental guarantees for the protection of personal rights." Nevertheless, the court went on, the determination of whether the right is to be exercised is not left to the defendant alone. The ultimate decision of the right to exercise the privilege is for the court.

In *In re Consolidated Rendering Co.* (1907) Consolidated was served with a subpoena duces tecum ordering it to produce certain records before a grand jury. The company refused and a contempt was found. In answer to its claim that the privilege of Article 10 protected the documents, the court referred to *Wigmore on Evidence*, which said:

> The question of relevancy is never one for the witness to concern himself with; nor is the applicability of a privilege to be left to his decision. It is his duty to bring what the court requires; and the court can then, to its own satisfaction, determine by inspection whether the documents produced are irrelevant or privileged.

It affirmed the contempt.

Not only are the documents of a corporation the possible subjects of Article 10 protection, but so are the papers of private individuals, as *State v. Slamon* (1901) held. There papers were taken from the person accused of a crime. "The seizure of a person's private papers to be used in evidence against him is equivalent to compelling him to be a witness against himself and in a prosecution for a crime is within the constitutional prohibition."

While in custody in a New Mexico jail awaiting extradition to Vermont, the defendant in *State v. Killary* (1975) made statements to an undercover narcotics informer who was in jail to "protect his cover." Killary admitted that he shot his wife and stated that he was going to "kill the officers holding him on his return trip to Vermont, or else slice his wrists and plead insanity." Prior to trial Killary moved to suppress the statements, claiming that the statements violated his constitutional right against self-incrimination as it related to his defense of insanity.

The court held that when a defendant initiates a dialogue with one who had no knowledge of the defendant or his alleged acts and is of a casual, gratuitous type, he cannot claim custodial interrogation and a resultant violation of his right against self-incrimination.

In *State v. Miner* (1969) the defendant was accused of killing his wife. He was committed to the Vermont State Hospital for examination as to his sanity. The state's psychiatrist testified that he had a conversation with the accused in the course of his examination at the hospital. The conversation was conducted without either threat or promise. Information obtained from the accused was "volunteered in back and forth conversation." No *Miranda* warning was given.

In the course of the conversation, the psychiatrist asked Mr. Miner why he was there. The reply was that it was because he had shot his wife. He had intended only to frighten her, but she started to run. "He said, if she hadn't started to run, he wouldn't have shot her." This conversation was allowed in evidence over the objection of the defendant.

The court held that the case must be retried as "the respondent's conversation with the state psychiatrist in the circumstances [is] proscribed by boundaries imposed in our federal and state constitutions. US Cons. Amend V and XIV, VT Const. Ch. I, Art. 10."

In the *Badger* case (1982) it was held that a second confession cannot be admissible if a product of a prior illegally obtained confession. Whether the second confession should be suppressed as a product of the first confession depends upon two elements. The first is causation. The second is whether intervening events break the causal chain. In *Badger* the court held that even the intervening *Miranda* warning would not purge the taint of illegality of the first confession.

That a confession must be voluntary to be admitted in evidence, of course, dates back to the Magna Carta. In *State v. Hobbs & Strong* (1803) the defendants coerced a confession from one Jenkins. Strong was acquitted and Hobbes was convicted. After reciting Article 10 of the Declaration of Rights with emphasis on the self-incrimination clause, the court said, "All compulsory process to enforce an acknowledgement of guilt is forever excluded, not only from our judicial proceedings, but all attempts of individuals to extort confession by bodily suffering [are] reprobated." Although never tested, it would seem that mental torture would stand in the same light as physical.

The right is a personal right available only to the witness. In *State v. Crepeault* (1967) the defendant was convicted on the testimony of three young accomplices. He claimed that their evidence of complicity was in violation of their constitutional rights against self-incrimination. The court said that the defendant could not assert the constitutional rights of another. Self-incrimination is a personal right and beyond the control of another person.

Nor is it a violation to compel a witness to answer questions relating to the truthfulness of previous testimony (*In re Mackenzie*, 1927).

Much has been written about alcohol related crimes. One method used to inhibit persons from drinking and driving is the so-called implied consent laws. In Vermont the question of a sobriety test of blood or breath was alleged to be in violation of the privilege against self-incrimination. The court has allowed evidence of a refusal to take the test to be admitted in evidence (*State v. Brean*, 1978, and *State v. Welch*, 1978). It had been held earlier that it was not a violation of Article 10 to take blood to determine whether a person was driving while intoxicated (*State v. Pierce*, 1958).

Does the privilege protect one against the admission of handwriting examples? According to *State v. Picknell* (1982), the answer is no.

Evidence previously suppressed may be introduced if the defendant testifies. The court has held "that admission of previously suppressed evidence to impeach credibility implicates a defendant's constitutional right to testify in his own defense. The defendant must choose between not testifying, and thus foregoing the opportunity to present his account of the incident, or testifying, and running the risk of being impeached with illegally obtained evidence" (*State v. Brunelle*, 1987).

As technology becomes more available, defendants' claims for its use become more insistent. In *State v. Gorton* (1988) the defendant argued that Article 10 should be so interpreted that police officers would be required to tape-record all inculpatory statements made by a criminal suspect while in custody. The court refused to so order, saying that the legislature was the body to augment citizens' due process rights.

LAW OF THE LAND: DUE PROCESS

Although the words "due process" are not to be found in Article 10, the words "law of the land" are found. The Vermont Supreme Court has, in effect, declared the terms to be synonymous. "The principle, that no man shall be deprived of his liberty or property, except by the 'law of the land,' or its synonym, 'due process of law,' is older than written constitutions, older even than Runnymede; and breathes so palpably the spirit of exact justice, that it needs no formulation in the organic law" (*Quimby v. Hazen*, 1881).

The defendant, a guardian, was charged with embezzlement from his ward. He objected that the statute violated the due process clauses of both the federal and state constitutions. The court held (*State v. Stewart*, 1981) that the due process standard to be used to measure a criminal statute is whether the statute "gives a person of ordinary intelligence fair notice that his conduct is forbidden."

"It is inconceivable to us that the defendants failed to understand that conversion to one's own use of payroll checks and funds from the trust accounts of incompetent wards would not constitute criminal actions."

Are there instances where hearings are not required? *In re Saucier* (1961) was a case where Saucier had been granted a pardon upon certain conditions. It further provided that "upon the consideration of the Governor for the time being (whose judgment shall be conclusive as to the fact) that you have violated and failed to perform the foregoing conditions this pardon shall become void." Saucier was apprehended on a governor's warrant based on a determination by a later governor that Saucier had violated the conditions of his pardon. Saucier claimed that the warrant did not specify the condition broken. The court held that the conditional pardon was "an act of grace or favor upon the part of the State by its Governor, and might be revoked without notice to the convict and without giving him an opportunity to be heard." So, too, a finding of temporary insanity by two physicians need not be by hearing. When, however, the restraint is to be made permanent, then a full-scale hearing must be held or there will be a violation of Article 10's due process clause (*In re Cornell*, 1941). See also *In re Allen* (1909).

PUBLIC TRIAL

The defendant is guaranteed a public trial by Article 10. A court may, in its discretion, protect a witness by excluding particular persons from the courtroom (*State v. Rusin*, 1989).

Article 11

Search and Seizure

> That the people have a right to hold themselves, their houses, papers, and possessions, free from search or seizure; and therefore warrants, without oath or affirmation first made, affording sufficient foundation for them, and whereby any officer or messenger may be commanded or required to search suspected places, or to seize any person or persons, his, her or their property, not particularly described, are contrary to that right, and ought not to be granted.

This article was taken almost verbatim from the Pennsylvania Constitution of 1776. It will be noted that the word "unreasonable," which is contained in the Fourth Amendment to the United States Constitution, does not appear in this article of the Vermont Constitution.

While Article 11 has been denoted the search and seizure article, it also is the basis for all informations filed by a prosecuting officer being under oath. In *State v. Donaldson* (1929) the state's attorney of Orleans County signed some informations in blank and left them with the municipal judge. The judge's secretary filled out the complaint without the presence of the state's attorney. Donaldson offered to show that the signed warrant was left with the judge not with the idea of a complaint against him (Donaldson) but for the convenience of the court if occasion required a prosecution of any kind.

The court held that "due process of law requires that the official signature must be attached to the charge actually made, which means ordinarily that it must be attached after the charge has been written in." If the facts indicated by the officers were true, there was no process, and the court was without jurisdiction.

However, where a warrant was properly prepared under the oath of the state's attorney, an amended complaint without the oath will not be fatal. The defect could be waived by going to trial without raising the question (*State v. Anderson*, 1956).

Vermont holds that an official complaint whereby a prosecution for crime commences cannot issue until the prosecuting officer is satisfied that the party charged is probably guilty (*In re Davis*, 1966). A person cannot be subject to arrest on an unfounded warrant so that he may be at the disposal of the authorities while a case is built against him. See also *State v. Woodmansee* (1970).

In *State v. Harre* (1937) the defendant was arraigned on an information properly prepared and signed by one Webster, then state's attorney of Franklin County. A jury trial resulted in a disagreement. Before a new trial was had, Webster retired, and his successor dismissed all counts in the original complaint and attempted to amend that complaint by adding thirty-three additional counts. The new state's attorney never signed the amended complaint. The court held that while amendments are permitted, nevertheless when the original counts had been deleted there was no complaint left to amend, and the new state's attorney had to proceed as if it were a new complaint and comply with Article 11.

A court could permit an amendment that would make the complaint show on its face what was the fact. In *State v. Freeman* (1887) the court approved an amendment permitted by a lower court which allowed the certificate of a notary who administered the oath to be appended to the complaint. As the court said: "The amendment did not change the body of the complaint, or touch any allegation in it, or affect the amount or kind of proof required. It simply made the complaint show on its face what it was in fact."

SEARCH AND SEIZURE

To have standing to challenge the search and seizure, Vermont has departed from the federal test. The Vermont test is set out in *State v. Wood* (1987). There the court held that "a defendant need only possessory, proprietary or participatory interest in the item seized to establish standing." It is necessary that the property or person to be seized be particularly described. In *Lincoln v. Smith* (1855) a warrant was issued "to search the premises described in the foregoing complaint, and if any intoxicating liquor should be found therein, under circumstances warranting the belief, that it was intended for sale, contrary, . . . to prevent the traffic in intoxicating liquor."

The return showed that the dwelling house was searched and one barrel of rum and eight barrels of cider were found "under such circumstances as warranted the belief that the same was kept for sale." Upon a finding by the court of its belief that the rum was intended for sale, it was declared forfeit and ordered destroyed. The court held that property may be described as nearly as may be. "If the liquor had been described, by a designation of its particular kind, or species, instead of using the generic term, it is difficult to see how this would have given more certainty; and besides in most cases it would be impractical." In this case the court pointed out the similarity of the Vermont and United States constitutions except for the word "unreasonable."

Where a search warrant authorized the search of a person for stolen goods, a personal letter found on the person could not be taken. Nor could the letter be used in evidence against the person. Such was the holding in the case of *State v. Slamon* (1901). Here was the exclusionary rule first enunciated in Vermont.

Although the word "unreasonable" is not present in Article 11, the court has permitted exceptions to the absolute rule against warrantless searches and seizures. In *State v. Badger* (1982) the court concluded its discussion of the Vermont constitutional issues by analyzing Article 11 as it applied to a pair of bloodstained shoes owned by the defendant and seized before an illegal confession was obtained. It concluded that as the police had employed the least restrictive method to obtain manifestly incriminating evidence and the vulnerable evidence was openly displayed, with no attempt at concealment, Article 11 was not violated. In *State v. Record* (1988) the word "unreasonable" was declared implicit in this article. A motor vehicle sobriety checkpoint was permitted if operated under rigid conditions.

Under the fish and game laws of Vermont, the game wardens are, by statute, given the authority to seize and search without warrant "where they have reason to believe that fish, birds or quadrupeds are possessed" in violation of the fish and game laws. A warden seized a car as evidence. "Our court held that as no claim was made that the vehicle was transporting illegal game at the time of seizure, Article 11 had been violated" (*State v. Aldrich*, 1961).

The article is designed to protect people, not places (*State v. Zaccaro*, 1990). It extends to the curtilage of a residence (*State v. Potter*, 1987).

Random prison cell searches have been held valid even though without a warrant. In *State v. Berard* (1990) the court seems to have adopted a balancing test with a "special needs" standard. There the court set out a three-pronged standard for prison searches.

Any violation of this article brings into play the federal exclusionary rule (*United States v. Pforzheimer*, 1987).

In *State v. Kirchoff* (1991) the Vermont court rejected the "open fields" doctrine of *Oliver v. United States* (1984). A defendant had posted no trespassing signs and other indicia of privacy in a patch of marijuana in a field away from his home. The court said, in reversing a conviction, that "we now hold that a lawful possessor may claim privacy in 'open fields' under Article XI of the Vermont

Constitution where indicia would lead a reasonable person to conclude that the area is private."

And in *State v. Oakes*(1991) the "good faith" exception to the exclusionary rule adopted by the United States Supreme Court was rejected by the Vermont Supreme Court.

Following *Kirchoff,* the court rejected the automobile container exception to the warrant rule of *California v. Acevedo* (1991). Vermont in *State v. Saava* (1991) declared that a closed container found in an automobile stopped by police cannot be searched without a warrant.

In *State v. Blow* (1991) the defendant appealed a conviction of dispensing marijuana. An informant was equipped with an electronic audio transmitter. He went to the defendant and purchased some marijuana. The conversation during the sale was monitored by a police detective. The court held that the defendant expected privacy in his own home and therefore the exclusionary rule, while not applicable under the Fourth Amendment, was applicable under Article 11.

The court held that, conversely, there was no expectation of privacy in a conversation held in a parking lot (*State v. Brooks,* 1991).

Article 12

Trial by Jury

That when any issue in fact, proper for the cognizance of a jury is joined in a court of law, the parties have a right to trial by jury, which ought to be held sacred.

The words "proper for the cognizance of a jury" have limited the right of parties to a jury trial for the findings of fact. The court in *State Dept. of Taxes v. Tri-State Industrial Laundries* (1980) stated that "this provision [Article 12] does not extend the right of trial by jury, but merely secures it to the extent that it existed at common law," citing *Dempsey v. Hollis* (1950).The *Dempsey* case was on a motion for a certified close jail execution (now outlawed). It was held that such a motion was independent of, as well as incidental and collateral to, the principal judgment and therefore no jury was constitutionally required. So in book account no jury is guaranteed. Jury trial was not demandable in an action of book account (*Hall v. Armstrong*, 1893) or insolvencies (*Crampton v. Hollister*, 1898). Courts of admiralty, equity, or probate did not, at common law, try their issues of fact before juries. Therefore, appeals from their decisions were not heard before juries but before the court (*In re Welch's Will*,1896).

This is not to say that rights established by statute after the adoption of the constitution would be heard without a jury:

All the rights, whether then or thereafter arising, which would properly fall into those classes of rights to which by the course of the common law the trial by jury was

> secured, were intended to be embraced within this article. Hence it is not the time when the violated right first had its existence, nor whether the statute which gives rise to it was adopted before or after the constitution that we are to regard as the criterion of the extent of this provision of the constitution; but it is the nature of the controversy between the parties, and its fitness to be tried by a jury according to the rules of the common law that must decide the question. (*Plimpton v. Somerset*, 1860).

When a trial by jury is guaranteed, the right cannot be violated. In *Shapiro v. Gore* (1934) the plaintiff proceeded at law on one promissory note. He also proceeded in equity to foreclose a mortgage securing the debt on two other notes. The chancellor in the foreclosure proceeding ordered the lawsuit transferred to his court and made part of the foreclosure action. The court held that this violated Article 12 and reversed the decree. The court declared:

> The plaintiff's action at law was triable by jury; the right to such a trial was guaranteed to him by Article 12 of our Bill of Rights. No court can lawfully deprive one so situated of this fundamental right. Nor can a Legislature so extend the jurisdiction of chancery as to cover and draw to it such a cause of action and give the court of chancery the right and power to determine it without the aid of a jury.

The jury referred to in Article 12 is the common law jury of twelve persons (*Rules of Procedure 23b and Rule 48 of Rules of Civil Procedure*).

Selecting juries guaranteed under Article 12 was the subject of the opinion in *State v. Mercier* (1925). The court said that the method of listing and selecting juries was within the authority of the legislature. The limitation is that the legislature cannot impair the right.

In a civil case arising from an automobile accident, *Harrington v. Decker* (1976), it was held that the parties have a right to be present at the drawing of the jury. However, if they receive notice and fail to appear, they have waived that right unless they can show an inability to be present and prejudice resulting therefrom.

Article 13

Freedom of Speech and of the Press

That the people have a right to freedom of speech, and of writing and publishing their sentiments, concerning the transactions of government, and therefore the freedom of the press ought not to be restrained.

Freedom of speech, and of the press, is guaranteed by the First Amendment to the United States Constitution. Article 13 was adopted by Vermont in its 1777 Constitution. It is also a longer article than the protection given in the First Amendment. However, the cases of free speech and press were generally argued through the First Amendment rather than Article 13.

The Vermont Supreme Court has held that there is a similarity between the two constitutional provisions but reserves judgment on whether greater scope is to be accorded to Article 13 (*In re Grievance of Morrissey*, 1987).

Defendant Stella Greaves was an ordained minister of the Jehovah's Witnesses. As such, she distributed the *Watchtower* and *Consolation* magazines published by the sect, for a fee of five cents, to any person wishing to obtain one. The city of Rutland had an ordinance prohibiting peddling without a license. Greaves was charged with violating that ordinance. She was found guilty after a jury trial. On appeal she claimed that her right to free speech and free press accorded her under the First Amendment as applied to the states by the Fourteenth Amendment had been violated (*State v. Greaves*, 1941).

In its opinion the court pointed out that the fee would impose a restraint on the defendant in distributing material which was fully protected under the

First Amendment. Citing from *Grosjean v. American Press Co.*, 297 U.S. 233 (1936), the court set out the history of taxation of the press and the evils that could flow from such action, "and that by the First Amendment it was meant to preclude the national government, and by the Fourteenth Amendment to preclude the states, from adopting any form of previous restraint upon printed publications or their circulation."

The question as to whether a reporter could be compelled to testify about the sources of his information without violating his First Amendment rights was answered in the affirmative in *State v. St. Peter* (1974). However, qualifications were placed upon the answer. The court said that a newsman, legitimately entitled to the First Amendment protection, may refuse to answer "unless the interrogator can demonstrate. . . that there is no other adequately available source for the information and that it is relevant and material on the issue of guilt or innocence."

In juvenile proceedings, however, the First Amendment right of access must be weighed against the confidentiality of juvenile proceedings. In *In re J. S.* (1981) the juvenile, J. S., had allegedly been involved with another youth in the assault and murder of one young girl and the assault on another young girl who was left for dead but survived. The court held that juvenile proceedings were not criminal. It further held that there were many reasons why the compelling interest in the confidentiality of juvenile proceedings would override the countervailing interests of the public and press in disseminating information that its reporters learn while attending the proceedings. It refused the request of the media to attend the hearing.

In pretrial proceedings in a criminal case the result was different. There a closure of a pretrial hearing was reversed (*Herald Association v. Ellison*, 1980). The majority in that case held that the policy of the state was against closure. Before a pretrial closure could be imposed, the trial court must consider all the procedural devices that would guarantee defendant a fair trial such as continuance, severance, change of venue, change of venire, voir dire, peremptory challenges, sequestration, and admonition of the jury, all as set out by Justice Blackmun in *Gannett Co. v. De Pasquale* (1979).

The court was faced with the issue of a public employee's First Amendment rights. The then editor of the magazine *Vermont Life*, Charles Morrissey, was dismissed from his position. *Vermont Life* is a division within the state of Vermont's Agency of Development and Community Affairs. Morrissey appealed his discharge to the State Labor Relations Board, claiming, among other reasons, that the dismissal violated his free speech rights under either the state or federal constitution.

The court agreed that a state employee does not lose his First Amendment right to comment on matters of public interest even when those matters involve the institution in which he is employed. The right, continued the court, is not absolute. There must be a balance between the interests of the employee as a citizen in commenting on those matters of public concern, and the state's interest, as an employer, in promoting the efficiency of the services it performs for the public through its employees. In the *Morrissey* case the court balanced in favor of the state on the facts of the case.

In *Blouin v. Anton* (1981) two politicians engaged in a war of words. The defendant called the plaintiff words which could be called insulting, abusive, unpleasant, and objectionable. The holding was that the defendant was speaking in hyperbole and as such the words were protected by Article 13.

Article 14

Immunity in Legislative Debate

The freedom of deliberation, speech, and debate in the Legislature, is so essential to the rights of the people, that it cannot be the foundation of any accusation or prosecution, action or complaint, in any other court or place whatsoever.

This article first appeared in the Constitution of 1786 and was carried into the Constitution of 1793. It predates the privilege accorded members of Congress in Section 6 of Article 1 of the federal constitution. There have been no cases decided by the court interpreting this article.

Article 15

Suspension of Laws by Legislature

> The power of suspending laws, or the execution of laws, ought never to be exercised but by the Legislature, or by authority derived from it, to be exercised in such particular cases as this constitution, or the Legislature shall provide for.

This article first appeared in the Constitution of 1786 and was carried with little amendment into the Constitution of 1793. There have been no cases decided by the court interpreting this article.

Article 16

Right to Bear Arms; Standing Armies; Military Power Subordinate to Civil

> That the people have a right to bear arms for the defence of themselves and the State—and as standing armies in time of peace are dangerous to liberty, they ought not to be kept up; and that the military should be kept under strict subordination to and governed by the civil power.

Does this article give to Vermonters an absolute right to carry arms? By statute, a person may not carry in a car or on a public highway a loaded rifle or shotgun. This was part of the fish and game laws of the state.In *State v. Duranleau* (1969) the court held that the restriction conditioned the unrestrained carrying and operation of firearms. Nevertheless, they went on to say, "But the language of the constitutional provision does not suggest that the right to bear arms is unlimited and undefinable." Here the right to bear arms was not unconstitutionally infringed.

Article 17

Martial Law

That no person in this state can, in any case be subjected to law-martial or to any penalties or pains by virtue of that law except those employed in the army, and the militia in actual service.

This article was incorporated into the constitution in 1786. It guarantees that no martial law will be imposed by the state on its citizens not in the army or in the militia in actual service. No cases have been decided by the court interpreting this article.

Article 18

Fundamental Principles and Virtues Necessary to Preserve Liberty

That frequent recurrence to fundamental principles, and a firm adherence to justice, moderation, temperance, industry and frugality, are absolutely necessary to preserve the blessings of liberty, and keep government free; the people ought, therefore to pay particular attention to these points, in the choice of officers and representatives, and have a right, in a legal way, to exact a due and constant regard to them, from their legislators and magistrates, in making and executing such laws as are necessary for the good government of the State.

This article was adopted verbatim from the Pennsylvania Declaration of Rights. The article was changed by the addition of the words "in a legal way" in the Constitution of 1786 and then continued in the Constitution of 1793. It is a warning to the freemen to be careful in electing their officials and a statement of the principles by which citizens will remain free.

This article by implication prohibits cruel and unusual punishments or excessive fines (*State v. Burlington Drug Co.*, 1911). See also Chapter 2, Section 40.

Article 19

Right to Emigrate

That all people have a natural and inherent right to emigrate from one State to another that will receive them.

The Constitution of 1777 contained additional language as follows: "or to form a new State in vacant countries, or in such countries as they can purchase, whenever they think that thereby they can promote their own happiness." This provision of the 1777 Constitution was taken directly from the Pennsylvania Declaration of Rights. The language was excised in the 1786 Constitution. No cases have been decided by the court interpreting this article.

Article 20

Right to Assemble, Instruct, and Petition

That the people have a right to assemble together to consult for their common good—to instruct their Representatives—and to apply to the Legislature for redress of grievances, by address, petition or remonstrance.

This article was adopted verbatim in 1777 from the Pennsylvania Declaration of Rights. It has remained without change since then.

"If this right of petitioning for a redress of grievances should sometimes be perverted—the right of petitioning with impunity is established both by common law and our declaration of rights, the abuse of the right must be submitted to in common with other evils in government, as subservient to the public welfare" (*Harris v. Huntington,* 1802). In the *Harris* case the defendants petitioned the General Assembly of the state to deny reappointment as a justice of the peace to Harris, who claimed that the petition was libellous. The jury had awarded Harris $1,000; the court reversed.

The *Harris* case was cited with approval in the case of *In re Petitions of Davenport et al.* (1971). One of the petitions concerned a teacher who had helped students prepare a petition requesting release time to have discussions in protest of the nation's involvement in the Vietnam War and Cambodia in particular. Her school board dismissed her for "conduct unbecoming a teacher."

The court held that the term was a catchall used where no specific other reason could be given. It is valid, said the court, when applied to serious cases of misconduct not protected by constitutional safeguards. The court concluded that the conduct of the teacher deserved constitutional protection.

There have been no cases interpreting other aspects of this article.

Article 21

No Transportation for Trial

That no person shall be liable to be transported out of this State for trial for any offence committed within the same.

This does not appear in the Pennsylvania Declaration of Rights of 1776. It has not been judicially interpreted.

2 Plan or Frame of Government

DELEGATION AND DISTRIBUTION OF POWERS

SECTION 1. GOVERNING POWER

The Commonwealth or State of Vermont shall be governed by a Governor (or Lieutenant Governor), a Senate and a House of Representatives of the freemen of the same, in manner and form following:

When this section was first adopted in the Constitution of 1777, the government consisted of a "Governor, Deputy-Governor, Council and the Assembly of Representatives of Freemen of the same." The language was taken verbatim from the Pennsylvania Constitution of 1776. The Constitution of 1786 changed deputy-governor to its present lieutenant-governor. Not until the 1836 convention adopted Amendments 3 and 8 to the Constitution of 1793 did the Senate replace the Governor's Council. There has been no litigation concerning this section.

SECTION 2. SUPREME LEGISLATIVE POWER

The Supreme Legislative power shall be exercised by a Senate and a House of Representatives.

This section originally did not contain provisions for a Senate. It rested the legislative power solely, as did its Pennsylvania model, in a House of Representatives. The Senate was established in 1836 and was included in this section through Amendment 3 to the Constitution of 1793.

The legislative powers exercised by the Senate and House of Representatives are broad. They consist not only of those powers granted in Section 6 but also powers to delegate, within limits, at least "in intricate matters affecting the general welfare in natural resources, health, education and economics" (*Vermont Home Mortgage Credit Agency v. Montpelier National Bank,* 1970).

In the early history of our American governments it was expedient for legislatures to delegate to subordinate agencies many duties related to the application of laws. The complexity of modern life and ever burgeoning field of governmental activity have made such delegation a necessity. "Nevertheless, it still remains the rule both in state and in nation that such delegation of authority must not encroach upon the strictly legislative functions of the legislature" (*Village of Waterbury v. Melendy,* 1938).

When the delegation of authority is questioned, the facts of the particular case will be determinative. An administrative agency cannot legislate (*State v. Auclair,* 1939). "But it can confer upon the executive and judicial branches of government or grant to a subordinate agency, of its own creation, a wide discretion in the manner and method for the execution of statutes validly adopted" (*Village of Waterbury v. Melendy,* 1938).

SECTION 3. SUPREME EXECUTIVE POWER

The Supreme Executive power shall be exercised by a Governor, or in his absence, a Lieutenant-Governor.

The 1777 provision declared the executive power to be vested in a governor and council. In 1786 the provision for the lieutenant-governor to be the executive in the absence of the governor was added. With the advent of the Senate in 1836, the council was eliminated by Amendment 8 of that year. There has been no litigation concerning this section.

SECTION 4. JUDICIARY

The judicial power of the State shall be vested in a unified judicial system which shall be composed of a Supreme Court, a Superior Court, and such other subordinate courts as the General Assembly may from time to time ordain and establish.

The Constitution of 1777 contained a much simpler judicial section: "Courts of justice shall be established in every county in the state." Subsequent amendments created a much more extensive section.

Following the report of a committee appointed to examine the constitution as it referred to the judicial branch, the present language of Section 4 was developed. Its proposed revisions, adopted in 1974, involved not only this section but also new provisions of the judiciary in Sections 30 through 41. This section has not been judicially interpreted.

SECTION 5. DEPARTMENTS TO BE DISTINCT

> The Legislative, Executive, and Judiciary departments, shall be separate and distinct, so that neither exercise the powers properly belonging to the others.

No provision for a constitutional separation of powers was contained in either the Pennsylvania Constitution or the original Vermont Constitution. The first Council of Censors suggested that such provision be incorporated into the constitution because of the misuse by the legislature of powers that should normally be judicial. The convention of 1786 adopted what was then Section 6 (now Section 5).

> The provision for keeping the departments of government separate does not mean an absolute separation of functions, for if it did it would really mean that we are to have no government, whereas our Constitution was ordained for the establishment of efficient government. (*Sabre v. Rutland R.R. Co. et al.*, 1913)

As we have seen, it is not possible for such separation to be absolute, as there must be a certain amount of overlapping or blending of the powers exercised by the different departments (*Village of Waterbury v. Melendy*, 1938).

While there may be a certain overlapping of powers, nevertheless, functions peculiar to one branch or the other cannot be delegated. The determination of negligence is a judicial function and cannot be delegated to an administrative body (*Trybulski v. Bellows Falls Hydro-Electric Corp.*, 1941). Nor can a legislative function be usurped by the judiciary. Judicial legislation violates the separation of powers doctrine (*State v. Jacobs.*, 1984).

An attempt by the legislature retroactively to limit the court's jurisdiction over cases that had been filed prior to the enactment of a law was a legislative interference with the discharge of judicial functions in violation of Section 5 (*Solomon v. Atlantis Development Inc.*, 1984). This case also represents the prohibition against ex post facto laws in a civil case.

The doctrine of separation of powers was invoked in the case of *In re Constitutionality of House Bill* 88 (1949). There the governor had requested an opinion on a bill passed by the legislature and before him for signature. The act required the supreme court to render advisory opinions. The court used Section 5 to respectfully decline to issue such opinions.

The court also invoked Section 5 in cases of election disputes. Because Section 14 of the constitution places the power to judge the election and qualification of their own members in the legislative branch, it held that courts could not pass upon asserted checklist irregularities.

Legislative Department

SECTION 6. LEGISLATIVE POWERS

The Senate and the House of Representatives shall be styled, *The General Assembly of the State of Vermont.* Each shall have and exercise the like powers in all acts of Legislation; and no bill, resolution, or other thing, which shall have been passed by the one, shall have the effect of, or be declared to be, a law, without the concurrence of the other. *Provided,* That all Revenue bills shall originate in the House of Representatives, but the Senate may propose or concur in amendments, as on other bills. Neither House during the session of the General Assembly, shall, without the consent of the other, adjourn for more than three days, nor to any other place than that in which the two Houses shall be sitting; and in case of disagreement between the two Houses with respect to adjournment, the Governor may adjourn them to such time as he shall think proper. They may prepare bills and enact them into laws, redress grievances, grant charters of incorporation, subject to the provisions of section 69, constitute towns, boroughs, cities and counties; and they shall have all other powers necessary for the Legislature of a free and sovereign State; but they shall have no power to add to alter, abolish, or infringe any part of this Constitution.

This section as finally revised in 1974 has been the subject of interpretation dating back to 1825 (*Ward v. Barnard*). In that case the legislature passed a law freeing Barnard from close jail. The court referred to Section 9 (now Section 6) and set out in full the powers of the legislature. It concluded: "The authority to redress grievances, if not limited to proper and appropriate acts of legislation, would be giving the general assembly authority as boundless, as the complaints of the citizens against each other, are countless. A right was vested in Ward which could not be taken away from him by the legislature."

It does not follow that the legislature is prohibited from delegating some powers. Municipal corporations certainly can be granted legislative powers: "the general doctrine prohibiting the delegating of legislative authority has no application to the vesting in *political subdivisions* of power to govern matters which are local in scope" (*Village of Waterbury v. Melendy*, 1938). Boards are also authorized to act as administrators of legislative policy.

Among the powers of the legislature is the creating or abolishing of towns or counties. It also may have retrospective powers.

Revenue bills must, by this section, originate in the House. What is a "revenue bill"? The Vermont Supreme Court has adopted the rule that the term refers to those acts whose primary purpose is to raise revenues to meet the general expenses and obligations of government, and not to bills designed to create revenue incidental to other purposes (*Andrews v. Lathrop*, 1974).

That part of the section which prohibits adjournment of one house for more than three days without the consent of the other house has not been judicially interpreted. However, an attorney general's opinion (Biennial Report of the Attorney General, 1940–42) states that in computing time within which an act may or may not be done, if the period exceeds one week Sundays are included, otherwise Sunday is excluded. The period does not include the date or event from which the time begins to run.

The power of the legislature to constitute towns, boroughs, cities, and counties appears to be unlimited. In *Montpelier v. East Montpelier* (1856) it was held that "so far as their public and municipal franchises and existence are concerned, it has become a well settled principle in the courts of this country, that the legislature may exercise over them exclusive control, and constitutionally may enlarge, restrain, and even destroy their municipal existence, as the public interests may require."

Towns and other governmental units are extensions of the legislature itself. The legislature determines what powers shall devolve upon them. These powers may be added to, subtracted from, or eliminated entirely by the "convenience or caprice" of the legislature (*Town of Bennington v. Park et al.*, 1877).

Finally, the legislature may not delegate its powers to "constitute towns, boroughs, cities and counties." Prior to *In re Constitutionality of House Bill 88* advisory opinions were rendered by the supreme court. The governor was faced with a bill that permitted villages to be chartered, and city and village charters amended, by direct petition to the Public Service Commission, bypassing the legislature. He requested an opinion of the supreme court whether such a provision would be constitutional. The court held in the negative (*In re Municipal Charters*, 1913).

SECTION 7. BIENNIAL SESSIONS

The General Assembly shall meet biennially on the first Wednesday next after the first Monday of January, beginning in A.D. 1915.

Initially, the meeting of the House of Representatives was to be on the first Tuesday of September annually (Constitution of 1777). In 1870 legislative sessions became biennial, and in 1913 the present Section 7 came into being. The language of this section appears to be unambiguous and has never been litigated.

SECTION 8. DOORS OF GENERAL ASSEMBLY TO BE OPEN

The doors of the House in which the General Assembly of this Commonwealth shall sit, shall be open for the admission of all persons who behave decently, except only when the welfare of the State may require them to be shut.

This provision, taken directly from the Pennsylvania Constitution of 1776, prohibits the legislature from secret sessions except where the "welfare of the state" may require. The courts have never been asked to determine whether the general welfare required shutting the doors of the Vermont General Assembly.

It should be noted that Vermont has been designated "The Commonwealth or State of Vermont"(Section 1). Here the designation is commonwealth. This section has never been judicially interpreted.

SECTION 9. JOURNALS: YEAS AND NAYS

The votes and proceedings of the General Assembly shall be printed (when one-third of the members of either House think it necessary) as soon as convenient after the end of the session, with the yeas and nays of the House of Representatives on any question when required by five members, and of the Senate when required by one Senator (except where the votes shall be taken by ballot), in which case every member of either House shall have a right to insert the reasons of his vote upon the minutes.

This section was originally taken directly from the Pennsylvania Constitution, which provided that one-third of the members of the House of Representatives could demand a printed record weekly and also the ayes and nays. Amendment 31 in 1913 changed weekly to end of session and delineated that five members of the House or one member of the Senate could demand the ayes and nays of their respective chambers. This section has never been the subject of litigation.

SECTION 10. STYLE OF LAWS

The style of the laws of this State shall be, *It is hereby enacted by the General Assembly of the State of Vermont.*

The 1777 Constitution contained a much more elaborate provision adopted from the Pennsylvania Constitution. This section has never been judicially interpreted.

SECTION 11. GOVERNOR TO APPROVE BILLS; VETO PROCEEDINGS; NON-ACTION

Every bill which shall have passed the Senate and House of Representatives shall, before it becomes a law, be presented to the Governor; if he approves, he shall sign it; if not, he shall return it, with his objections in writing, to the House in which it shall have originated; which shall proceed to reconsider it. If, upon such reconsideration, two-thirds of the members present of that House shall pass the bill, it shall, together with the objections, be sent to the other House, by which it shall likewise be reconsidered, and, if approved by two-thirds of the members present of that House, it shall become a law.

But, in all such cases, the votes of both Houses shall be taken by yeas and nays, and the names of the persons voting for or against the bill shall be entered on the journal of each House, respectively. If any bill shall not be returned by the Governor, as aforesaid, within five days (Sundays excepted) after it shall have been presented to him, the same shall become a law in like manner as if he had signed it; unless the two Houses by their adjournment, within three days after the presentation of such bill shall prevent its return; in which case it shall not become a law.

Before the advent of the Senate in 1836, there was no veto power in the governor. Article of Amendment 11 in 1836 established the veto but permitted a majority in both houses to override it. The majority became two-thirds by an amendment passed in 1913.

In *Hartness v. Black* (1921) the secretary of state claimed that the governor could not validate any law sent him after adjournment of the legislature and cited Section 11. The court ruled that the determinative time was when the governor signed the act, not when it was messaged to him.

The legislature passed a resolution but failed to present it to the governor for his approval. The court held that the joint resolution was not a legal enactment. " The governor under the constitution of this State, is a co-ordinate branch of the government, and a necessary party to all 'acts of legislation'" (*Kellogg v. State Treasurer*, 1871).

In *National Land and Loan Co. v. Mead* (1888) the then governor submitted an affidavit stating that he had signed a bill and that his signature was timely.

He further stated that he approved of the bill but found that he had inadvertently signed the act in the wrong place. He erased his signature and, at a later date but much after the legislature had adjourned, had signed the bill at the proper place.

The court disposed of the matter by declaring that as long as the governor intended to sign the bill, the place of signing was incidental.

SECTION 12. FEES FOR ADVOCATING BILLS

> No member of the General Assembly shall, directly or indirectly, receive any fee or reward, to bring forward or advocate any bill, petition, or other business to be transacted in the Legislature; or advocate any cause, as counsel in either House of Legislation, except when employed in behalf of the State.

This provision was inserted in the basic Constitution of 1793 as Section 19 of Chapter 2.

Even though the second Council of Censors report does not indicate the reason for its inclusion, the reason seems clear on its face—to prevent corruption. The provision has never been judicially interpreted.

SECTION 13. NUMBER OF REPRESENTATIVES

> The House of Representatives shall be composed of one hundred and fifty Representatives. The freemen of each representative district established by law shall elect one or two Representatives from that district, the number from each district to be established by the General Assembly.
>
> In establishing representative districts, which shall afford equality of representation, the General Assembly shall seek to maintain geographical compactness and contiguity and to adhere to boundaries of counties and other existing political subdivisions.

This provision was the result of the one person, one vote doctrine set out in a series of United States Supreme Court decisions, commencing with *Baker v. Carr* (1962) and *Reynolds v. Sims* (1964). In the beginning each town having eighty inhabitants was entitled to two representatives; those having less had only one. Later each town was allowed one representative regardless of population.

This section as set out in the 1793 Constitution was declared unconstitutional in *Buckley v. Hoff* (1964) and affirmed and modified by the U.S. Supreme Court (1965). It was found that the House under the one representative from each town was grossly malapportioned and violated the equal protection clause of the Fourteenth Amendment to the United States Constitution.

The legislature reapportioned the House and Senate and established a plan for periodic reapportionment. It failed, however, to enact legislation for the election of a General Assembly to serve in January 1966 as directed. The federal court directed that elections be held on October 19, 1965, and November 29, 1965, and decreed that those persons elected would constitute the lawfully constituted legislature in 1966.

The plaintiff in *Hutchinson v. Cooley* (1965) claimed that the elections called for by the district court were invalid, alleging that the state court rather than the federal courts should establish all aspects of state reapportionment.

The Vermont court went on to say that if the litigation had come before it in the first instance, it would have had jurisdiction. That not having been done, the federal courts then did have jurisdiction. "If the constitution of a state stands in the way of prompt corrective action designed to achieve compliance with the Federal Constitution the state 'must amend it or yield to an authority that is paramount to the state' " (*Hutchinson v. Cooley*).

The attorney general has submitted an opinion that a constitutional convention could be called for the purpose of proposing amendments to the constitution. It was also his opinion that any proposals suggested by the convention must be submitted to the people for ratification or rejection (Biennial Report of the Attorney General, 1964–66).

SECTION 14. POWERS OF HOUSE

> The Representatives so chosen (a majority of whom shall constitute a quorum for transacting any other business than raising a State Tax, for which two-thirds of the members elected shall be present) shall meet as required by section 7, and shall be styled the House of Representatives: they shall have power to choose their Speaker, their Clerk and other necessary officers, sit on their own adjournments subject to the limitations of section 6, judge of the elections and qualifications of their own members; they may expel members, but not for causes known to their constituents antecedent to their election,administer oaths and affirmations in matters depending before them, and impeach state criminals.

This section originated as Section 8 of the Constitution of 1777.

In *Kennedy v. Chittenden* (1983) the supreme court struck down statutes that seemed to permit election contests to be heard by a superior court. The court stated that these statutes improperly delegated legislative powers to a separate branch of government, because Section 14 made the House of Representatives the "judge of the elections and qualifications of their own members."

SECTION 15. RESIDENCE OF REPRESENTATIVES AND SENATORS

No person shall be elected a Representative or a Senator until he has resided in this State two years, the last year of which shall be in the legislative district for which he is elected.

The Vermont Constitution of 1777 contained no residency requirement for a candidate for representative or senator. The 1793 Constitution required a two-year residence in the state, "the last of which shall be in the town for which he is elected" (Section 18). In 1974 the present language was adopted to conform the constitution to the reapportionment of the House and Senate.

The Vermont courts have held that the question of residence is a complex one. One must have an intent to have one's home in a particular place, but one must couple that intent with specific acts indicating that intent (*Fulham v. Howe*, 1890). It is also well settled that a person must have a residence somewhere. There have, however, been no supreme court decisions specifically interpreting this section.

SECTION 16. REPRESENTATIVES' OATHS

The Representatives having met, and chosen their Speaker and Clerk, shall each of them, before they proceed to business, take and subscribe, as well the oath or affirmation of allegiance hereinafter directed (except where they shall produce certificates of their having therefore taken and subscribed the same) as the following oath or affirmation, viz:

You——do solemnly swear (or affirm) that, as a member of this Assembly, you will not propose, or assent to, any bill, vote or resolution, which shall appear to you injurious to the people, nor do not consent to any act or thing whatever, that shall have a tendency to lessen or abridge their rights and privileges, as declared by the Constitution of this state; but will, in all things, conduct yourself as a faithful, honest, representative and guardian of the people, according to the best of your judgment and abilities. (In case of an oath) So help you God, (And in case of an affirmation) *under the pains and penalties of perjury.*

Initially, the Vermont Constitution required legislators to "own and profess the protestant religion." The 1793 Constitution excised this part of the oath, and the section remains without further amendment. The senators do not take an oath comparable to that prescribed by Section 16. Theirs is set out in 2 V.S.A. 3.

In his biennial report for 1966–68 the attorney general issued an opinion relative to the so-called unit rule, that is, a party rule. He stated that a representative voting pursuant to such rule would be in violation of his oath. There have been no supreme court decisions specifically interpreting this section.

SECTION 17. OATH OF SENATORS AND REPRESENTATIVES

The Representatives having met on the day appointed by law for the commencement of a biennial session of the General Assembly, and chosen their Speaker, and the Senators having met, shall, before they proceed to business, take and subscribe the following oath prescribed in the foregoing section:

You——do solemnly swear (or affirm) *that you did not at the time of your election to this body, and that you do not now, hold any office of profit or trust under the authority of Congress. So help you God.* (Or in case of an affirmation) *Under the pains and penalties of perjury.*

The words, "office of profit or trust under the authority of Congress" shall be construed to mean any office created directly or indirectly by Congress, and for which emolument is provided from the Treasury of the United States, other than that of a member of the commissioned or enlisted personnel in the reserve components of the armed forces of the United States while not on extended active duty.

This additional oath was first incorporated into the constitution through Article 27 of the amendments in 1883. That article, however, did not contain the exception relative to membership in the reserve components of the armed forces. That provision was added by Article 42 of the amendments (1954). The section has never been judicially interpreted.

SECTION 18. NUMBER AND QUALIFICATIONS OF SENATORS

The Senate shall be composed of thirty Senators to be of the freemen of the senatorial district from which they are elected. The freemen of each senatorial district established by law shall elect one or more Senators from that district, the number from each district to be established by the General Assembly.

In establishing senatorial districts, which shall afford equality of representation, the General Assembly shall seek to maintain geographical compactness and contiguity and to adhere to boundaries of counties and other existing political subdivisions.

Vermont had a unicameral legislature until 1836, when the present bicameral system was established (Article 3 of the amendments). Under Article 4 of the amendments (1836), thirty senators were chosen (the same as today), but each county was entitled to at least one senator.

In 1974 the present Section 18 was adopted as part of a sweeping change occasioned by the one person, one vote rule established by the United States Supreme Court. The biennial election of senators, however, had been established by Section 2 of Article of Amendment 24 (1870). Their term was now to be two years commencing on the first Wednesday of October following their election (Section 4). Their election was to be on the first Tuesday of September (Section 1).

The age requirement was eliminated as a qualification of a senator. By Article 47 (1974), persons of the age of eighteen "shall be entitled to all the privileges of a freeman of this state." Today any citizen eighteen years of age or older who meets a residency requirement set out by the legislature may be elected to the Senate of the state of Vermont.

SECTION 19. POWERS OF SENATE; LIEUTENANT-GOVERNOR'S DUTIES

The Senate shall have the like powers to decide on the election and qualifications of, and to expel any of its members, make its own rules, and appoint its own officers, as are incident to, or are possessed by, the House of Representatives. A majority shall constitute a quorum. The Lieutenant-Governor shall be President of the Senate, except when he shall exercise the office of Governor, or when his office shall be vacant, or in his absence, in which cases the Senate shall appoint one of its own members to be President of the Senate, *pro tempore*. And the President of the Senate shall have a casting vote, but no other.

This Section 19 became part of the constitution through Article 6 of the amendments (1836). It defines the powers and duties of the Senate as well as the establishment, duties, and powers of the president of the Senate. It has never been changed, nor has it been judicially interpreted.

Executive Department

SECTION 20. GOVERNOR; EXECUTIVE POWER

The Governor, and in his absence, the Lieutenant-Governor, shall have power to commission all officers, and also to appoint officers, except where provision is, or shall be, otherwise made by law or this Frame of Government; and shall supply every vacancy in any office, occasioned by death or otherwise, until the office can be filled in the manner directed by law or this Constitution. He is to correspond with other States; transact business with officers of government, civil and military, and prepare such business as may appear to him necessary, to lay before the General Assembly. He shall have power to grant pardons and remit fines in all cases whatsoever, except in treason in which he shall have power to grant reprieves, but not to pardon, until after the end of the next session of the General Assembly; and except in cases of impeachment, in which he shall not grant reprieve or pardon, and there shall be no remission, or mitigation of punishment, but by act of legislation. He is also to take care that the laws be faithfully executed. He is to expedite the execution of such measures as may be resolved upon by the General Assembly. And he may draw upon the Treasury for such sums as may be appropriated by the General Assembly. He may also lay embargoes, or prohibit the exportation of any commodity, for any time not exceeding thirty days, in the recess of the General Assembly only. He may grant such licenses as shall be directed by law; and shall have power to call together the General Assembly, when necessary, before the day to which they shall stand adjourned. The Governor shall be Captain-General and Commander-in-Chief of the forces of

> the State, but shall not command in person, in time of war, or insurrection unless by the advice and consent of the Senate, and no longer than they shall approve thereof. And the Lieutenant-Governor shall, by virtue of his office, be Lieutenant-General of all the forces of the State.

The Constitution of 1777 created the Governor's Council, which was abolished in 1836 when a bicameral legislature was instituted. The powers of the governor now set out in Section 20 are generally the same as those set out in the 1793 Constitution.

The governor has the power to appoint in any office in cases of vacancies. A vacancy occurring in the office of a United States Senator through resignation took a different direction. In that case the Constitution of the United States, Article XVII (the Seventeenth Amendment), controlled. That amendment authorized the legislature of a state to grant the executive power to appoint temporarily, otherwise the vacancy would remain until an election could be held. The Vermont legislature granted to the governor the power to appoint in case of death. This limitation by the legislature denied the governor the power to appoint in the case of a resignation (Biennial Report of the Attorney General, 1944–46). The attorney general reiterated this position in a subsequent letter to the governor (Biennial Report of the Attorney General, 1944–46).

In *In re St. Amour* (1969) the petitioner obtained a conditional pardon from the governor. Subsequent to his release, an executive warrant was issued founded upon his breach of conditions. No hearing was held, and he was incarcerated to complete his sentence. He now claimed that the actions of the governor in revoking the pardon without hearing violated the due process guaranteed by the state and federal constitutions. The court held that "no prisoner has a legal right to a conditional pardon. A conditional pardon is a grant, which becomes valid only on the acceptance of it by the convict, who can reject it, but who on accepting it takes it subject to all conditions in the grant. . . . Where a prisoner accepts a conditional pardon and voluntarily submits himself to the conditions stated therein, he is bound by them." "In the eye of the law, the conditionally pardoned convict is looked upon as being constantly in the custody of the Governor, who is regarded as his jailer, and has 'him always on a string that he may pull at pleasure.' . . . Such a pardon is bestowed on a prisoner as an act of grace or favor upon the part of the State by its Governor, and might be revoked without notice to the convict and without giving him an opportunity to be heard" (*In re St. Amour*, 1969).

The power to pardon cannot be delegated. In 1901 the then governor requested an opinion of the justices about certain legislative action which seemed to remove the pardoning power from the governor to a board. The legislature had also determined by statute that if a convict conditionally pardoned violated the conditions, he would be returned to commence his sentence as if he had never served any part thereof. The court held that pardoning, whether conditional or otherwise, could not be delegated but was a prerogative of the governor. The court also expressed its opinion that a convict could not be forced to recommence his sentence but could only complete the unserved portion of that sentence (*In re Conditional Discharge of Convicts*, 1901).

The petitioner in *In re De Palo* (1929) was granted a conditional pardon. If his released time were counted before he was returned to custody for breach of conditions, his sentence would have expired, and he so argued. The court, however, held that the time in which he had been at large was not to be treated as served upon his sentence.

The attorney general has held that the board of mental health could conditionally discharge (pardon) patients at the state hospital except those who have been convicted of a crime and ordered to a mental institution (Biennial Report of the Attorney General, 1944–46, p. 133). It has also been held that pardons are a matter of public record and thus subject to public scrutiny. The media requested the names of persons pardoned by the governor. The trial court issued an injunction against the media. The Vermont Supreme Court reversed, holding that pardons are public record (*Doe v. Salmon*, 1977).

A person convicted of adultery was sentenced and placed on probation. He subsequently applied to the governor for a pardon. The Department of Probation and Parole claimed that in that circumstance the governor could only issue an unconditional pardon. The attorney general issued an opinion (Biennial Report of the Attorney General, 1946–48) affirming that the governor could issue any kind of a pardon he wished. The attorney general cited *In re Conditional Discharge of Convicts*(1901) wherein it is stated:

> The power to grant pardons is given to the executive by the constitution in unrestricted terms, except in cases of treason, murder, and impeachment; and that such general power includes the authority to grant all kinds of pardon known to the common law, is well settled. The grant may be for a full, partial, absolute, or conditional pardon, provided the condition is not illegal, immoral, or impossible to perform. (*In re Conditional Discharge of Convicts*, 1901)

In the *De Palo* case, the maximum term of imprisonment under the original sentence expired, and the governor, who had issued a conditional pardon in the meantime, had not released the prisoner. The prisoner requested the court to declare the sentence terminated and the pardon discharged. The court held that his acceptance of the conditional pardon rendered him a subject of the governor until the governor excused him from the conditions (*In re De Palo*, 1929).

Can a judge remit a fine? The attorney general held in the negative (Biennial Report of the Attorney General, 1958–60) on the grounds that remission is pardoning, and pardoning is the exclusive power of the executive.

Does a pardon include the remission of costs where so assessed? Yes, answered the attorney general (Biennial Report of the Attorney General, 1940–42). Costs are a legal consequence of the conviction of guilt, and therefore a pardon would cancel such a consequence. He further opined that any costs that had been paid could not be recovered.

But is a license to operate a motor vehicle revoked by the commissioner of motor vehicles reinstated by a full pardon? Yes and no, said the attorney general. Yes, if the revocation is automatic. It then becomes part of the crime and is wiped out with the pardon. No, if the revocation is discretionary or if the legislature has invested the commissioner with the power after hearing and determining that a licensee is incompetent or an improper person to hold such license (Biennial Report of the Attorney General, 1934–36).

Can the courts review a pardon? The court held in the negative except as to questions of validity (*Doe v. Salmon*, 1977).

SECTION 21. SECRETARY OF CIVIL AND MILITARY AFFAIRS

> The Governor may have a Secretary of Civil and Military Affairs, to be by him appointed during pleasure, whose services he may at all times command; and for whose compensation provision shall be made by law.

This section in its present form was part of Article 8 of the amendments. It probably dates back to the 1777 Constitution where Section 18 provided in part for a secretary for the governor and council. Section 21 became a separate section under the authority of the supreme court of 1913 to revise Chapter 2 of the 1793 Constitution.

The section has been the subject of one opinion of the attorney general, although it has never been judicially tested. In his biennial report for 1950 the attorney general rendered an opinion that Section 21 did not conflict with Section 50, which set out incompatible offices.

SECTION 22. COMMISSIONS; STATE SEAL

> All commissions shall be in the name of *The Freemen of the State of Vermont*, sealed with the State Seal, signed by the Governor, and in his absence by the Lieutenant-Governor, and attested by the Secretary; which Seal shall be kept by the Governor.

This section came substantively from Section 21 of the Pennsylvania Constitution of 1776, incorporated in Section 19 of the 1777 Constitution of Vermont with the Governor's Council designated as the repository of the seal. This was carried over to the 1786 Constitution. The repository of the seal was designated as the governor in Section 22 of the Constitution of 1793, and the section has not been changed since that time. It has not been judicially reviewed.

SECTION 23. RESIDENCE OF GOVERNOR AND LIEUTENANT-GOVERNOR

No person shall be eligible to the office of Governor or Lieutenant-Governor until he shall have resided in this State four years next preceding the day of his election.

The Constitution of 1793 originated this residency requirement, and it has remained unchanged. This section has never been judicially reviewed.

SECTION 24. VACANCY IN OFFICE OF GOVERNOR, LIEUTENANT-GOVERNOR, AND TREASURER

The Legislature shall provide by general law what officer shall act as Governor whenever there shall be a vacancy in both the offices of Governor and Lieutenant-Governor, occasioned by a failure to elect, or by the removal from office, or by the death or resignation of both Governor and Lieutenant-Governor, or by the inability of both Governor and Lieutenant-Governor to exercise the powers and discharge the duties of the office of Governor; and such officer so designated shall exercise the powers and discharge the duties appertaining to the office of Governor accordingly until the disability shall be removed, or a Governor shall be elected. And in case there shall be a vacancy in the office of Treasurer, by reason of any of the causes enumerated, the Governor shall appoint a Treasurer for the time being, who shall act as Treasurer until the disability shall be removed, or a new election shall be made.

This section was part of Article of Amendment 21 adopted in 1850. Prior to that time, there was no constitutional provision for filling a vacancy if both the governor and lieutenant-governor were disqualified. With annual elections, there would be no urgency to replace a governor other than by the lieutenant-governor. It was not until 1870 that the elections became biennial. This section has not been judicially reviewed.

SECTION 25. SECURITY GIVEN BY TREASURER AND SHERIFFS

The Treasurer of the State shall, before entering upon the duties of his office, give sufficient security to the Secretary of State, in behalf of the State of Vermont, before the Governor of the State or one of the Justices of the Supreme Court. And Sheriffs, before entering upon the duties of their offices, shall give sufficient security in such manner and in such sums as shall be directed by the Legislature.

No bond was required of these officials until the Constitution of 1793. Then, by Section 27, the treasurer, "before the Governor and Council," was required to give security in behalf of the General Assembly, and the sheriffs "before the First Judge of the County Court, to the Treasurer of their respective counties." By Article of Amendment 22 (1850) the treasurer had to give his security before the governor or one of the judges of the supreme court. The sheriffs and high bailiffs (added in 1850) gave their security before "one of the Judges of the Supreme Court, or the two Assistant Judges of the County Court of their respective Counties." Addition of the assistant judges probably came about because by Article 14 (1850) they became, in effect, constitutional officers. By Article 46 (1974) the present language was adopted.

The question of the validity of the sheriffs bonds came before the court in the cases of *Taylor v. Nichols* (1856) and *Wing v. Gleason* (1863). In the *Taylor* case the sheriff had acted in that capacity for a year before he entered into a bond, and then before only one assistant judge. The court held that this was substantial compliance with the provision of Section 25.

In *Wing* the court pointed out that the amendment required action by the legislature. It held, therefore, that the statute in force remained until the legislature enacted new legislation as seemingly required by the constitutional amendment.

SECTION 26. TREASURER'S ACCOUNTS

The Treasurer's accounts shall be annually audited, and a fair state thereof laid before the General Assembly at its biennial session in January.

This section first appeared in the Constitution of 1786 as Section 25 and was carried forward into the Constitution of 1793 as Section 28. The only change made was to change the month from October in 1776 and 1793 to January in the present revision. This section has not been judicially reviewed.

SECTION 27. DRAWING MONEY FROM TREASURY

No money shall be drawn out of the Treasury, unless first appropriated by act of legislation.

This section first appeared in 1793 and has remained without change. The first case to test this section occurred after the establishment by the legislature of an emergency board, which was appropriated money to make any expenditures necessitated by unforeseen emergencies (*Grout v. Gates*, 1924). The legislature appropriated funds to the emergency board. The board, in turn, appropriated part of the funds to the secretary of state for use in the automobile department. The auditor of accounts refused to issue his warrant for payment of these amounts for the benefit of the secretary of state. The court held that the legislature could delegate to the emergency board funds without specific amounts for any unforeseen emergencies. In the instant case, however, they upheld the auditor because of the specific language of the authorization to the board. They held that the board itself must expend the money for the emergency.

In *City of Montpelier v. Gates et al.* (1933) certain payments were to be made to municipalities as reimbursement for loss in funds due to a change in the law. The specific sum for each town was to be determined independently of the general legislation, and warrants therefor were to be issued by the treasurer. The auditor refused to honor the certificates, claiming that the legislature had made no appropriation for the individual towns' amounts. The auditor further claimed that the moneys were not available, as the warrants were issued after the close of the fiscal year for which the appropriation had been made. The court made short shrift of the claims, holding that the section was not a restriction of the power of the legislature over public revenues. "It is the province of that body to cast the appropriation in a mould of its own making. . . . All that is essential is that the Legislature, by a valid enactment, shall assign to a particular use a sum of money from the public revenues" (*Grout v. Gates*, 1924). It also held that the moneys appropriated in one fiscal year were available in the next.

In *State Highway Board v. Gates* (1938) the *Montpelier v. Gates* case was used as authority for the emergency board to appropriate funds for emergencies.

A lien on funds coming into the state is not an appropriation, nor need it be appropriated. Governor Stanley Wilson properly entered into a contingent fee agreement with some attorneys. They were to receive 25 percent of any moneys recovered in a claim of the state against the United States. They were successful and claimed the money from the state. Based on an opinion from the attorney general, the auditor refused to allow the payment. The court held that a lien had been placed on the funds, and therefore the money for the fee never became part of the general fund of the state and was not, nor could it be, appropriated (*Button et al. v. Anderson et al.*, 1942).

Judiciary Department

SECTION 28. COURTS OF JUSTICE

The Courts of Justice shall be open for the trial of all causes proper for their cognizance; and justice shall be therein impartially administered, without corruption or unnecessary delay.

By certain sections of Article of Amendment 46 in 1974 the composition of the judiciary, its duties, powers, and limitations were set forth in full for the first time. They are designated in the revised Constitution of 1793 as Sections 28 through 37. The language in Section 28 originated in the 1776 Pennsylvania Constitution and was carried over into Section 23 of the 1777 Constitution of Vermont.

Through the years much was made of the lack of direction as to the judiciary in the 1793 Constitution, and change was thought to benecessary. Finally a commission was established to suggest constitutional amendments to the 1970 legislature. The major amendment was Article of Amendment 46.

In addition to the due process and fair trial protections granted litigants, the original Section 28 was set out in *Morse v. Ward* (1930): "that it is the duty of the court to conduct a trial with the utmost impartiality and fairness is elemental and fundamental" (*Morse v. Ward*) was reiterated in *State v. Hedding* (1961). In the leading case of *Leonard v. Willcox et al.* (1928) the court said that it was necessary to show bias or prejudice against a party before a judge could be disqualified. In an earlier case, *State v. Jurras* (1923), it was held that while the legislature could establish the municipal courts and describe their jurisdictions, the municipal judges were still subject to the provisions of Section 28.

In *Granai v. Witters* (1963) the court held as violative of Section 28 a statute that provided for the continuance of a civil trial if one of the attorneys was a member of the legislature during the legislative session.

Prior to the 1974 amendment this was Section 4 of the 1793 Constitution. This section has been declared to make the courts available to appeals from the orders of administrative bodies to test whether their powers have been exceeded (*Sabre v. Rutland Railroad Co.*, 1913).

While the section calls for justice "without corruption or unnecessary delay," a sentence reconsideration is not included.

In *Fleury v. KessellDuff Construction Co.* (1988) the plaintiff, Fleury, had been granted attorneys' fees following a successful claim for worker's compensation. The defendant did not object to the amount of the fees but claimed that the allowance for the plaintiff but not for the defendant forced the employer to purchase justice in violation of Section 28. The court summarily dismissed this claim.

SECTION 29. COMPOSITION OF SUPREME COURT

The Supreme Court shall consist of the Chief Justice of the State and four associate justices of the Supreme Court.

This section was incorporated into the constitution through Article of Amendment 46. It marked the first time the constitution set out the specific number of supreme court judges. This section has not been judicially reviewed.

SECTION 30. JURISDICTION OF SUPREME COURT

The Supreme Court shall exercise appellate jurisdiction in all cases, criminal and civil, under such terms and conditions as it shall specify in rules not inconsistent with law. The Supreme Court shall have original jurisdiction only as provided by law, but it shall have the power to issue all writs necessary or appropriate in aid of its appellate jurisdiction. The Supreme Court shall have administrative control of all the courts of the state, and disciplinary authority concerning all judicial officers and attorneys at law in the State.

The court has, since Section 30 was adopted in 1974, passed upon the disciplining and readmission of disbarred attorneys. In the case of *In re Harrington* (1976) the court readmitted to practice an attorney who had been disbarred following his conviction for extortion. His petition was filed with the Professional Conduct Board, and the board panel recommended, with one dissenter, that the petition for readmission be denied. The Court, however, declared that although the recommendation would be given great weight, the court would make the final decision. "The only final and ultimate decision is made here, on the responsibility of this Court." Harrington was readmitted to practice.

SECTION 31. JURISDICTION OF LOWER COURTS

> All other courts of this State shall have original and appellate jurisdiction as provided by law. All courts except the Supreme Court may be divided into geographical and functional divisions as provided by law or by judicial rules adopted by the Supreme Court not inconsistent with law. The jurisdiction of geographical and functional divisions shall be as provided by law or by judicial rules not inconsistent with law. The courts of this state may exercise equity jurisdiction as well as law jurisdiction in civil proceedings as may be provided by law or by judicial rules not inconsistent with law.

This section was added as part of Article of Amendment 46. It does not guarantee any specific number of superior court judges, nor does it guarantee the existence of any superior courts. It does, however, grant to the supreme court by rule the power to establish "geographical" and "functional" divisions of those courts.

The whole power does not, however, reside in the supreme court. The phrase "not inconsistent with law" infers that the court must be bound either by the constitution or by the constitution and laws passed by the legislature. The rule-making power of the court (see Constitution, Section 37) may be restricted by the legislature. The language "not inconsistent with law" would seem to indicate the possibility of conflict between the two bodies.

Until the amendments in 1974 the judiciary was apparently a subservient branch of government. Its budget was not submitted by the court but by the attorney general. It is now a part of the governor's budget proposal. Very little suggested legislation was offered by the court. Elections of judges were held biennially each session of the legislature (Article of Amendment 26, 1870). Until 1870 the elections were held annually by the legislature.

The rotation of the superior court judges around the state was determined by the judges themselves (*Ketchum v. Lehner*, 1988), but the legislature appointed the various terms of the county courts. The terms of the county courts (now superior courts) were established by statute.

SECTION 32. FILLING JUDICIAL VACANCIES

> The Governor, with the advice and consent of the Senate, shall fill a vacancy in the office of Chief Justice of the State, associate Justice of the Supreme Court or judge of any other court, except the office of Assistant Judge and of Judge of Probate, from a

list of nominees presented to him by a judicial nominating body established by the General Assembly having authority to apply reasonable standards of selection.

This section is a radical departure from the method of selection previously followed. Vermont's earliest constitution gave to the governor and council the power to "appoint and commission all officers (except those who are appointed by the General Assembly)."

However, from 1786 onward the election of judges was in the hands of the General Assembly, initially in conjunction with the council, and after 1836 jointly with the Senate.

After the legislature established the district court and set out territorial districts, a vacancy occurred on the district bench. The retiring judge was a resident of one geographical unit. The court reassigned a judge living in another unit to the vacant unit. The court held that the power of assignment was in the supreme court (*Ketchum v. Lehner*, 1988).

SECTION 33. INTERIM JUDICIAL APPOINTMENTS

When the Senate is not in session, the Governor may make an interim appointment to fill a vacancy in the office of chief justice, associate justice of the Supreme Court or judge of any other court, except the office of Assistant Judge and of Judge of Probate, from a list of nominees presented by the judicial nominating body. A justice or judge so appointed shall hold office, with all the powers incident to the office, until the Senate convenes and acts upon the appointment submitted by the Governor. Thereafter, the appointee shall continue in office if the Senate consents to the appointment. If the appointment is not confirmed upon vote of the Senate, the appointment shall be terminated and a vacancy in the office will be created.

Again, this marks a radical change in the method of filling a vacancy in the judiciary. The 1777 Vermont Constitution assigned this responsibility to the governor and council. When the council was eliminated in 1836, then by Article of Amendment 8 the governor assumed all powers and duties of the council. This carried through to Article of Amendment 46, which gave us the present Section 33.

The power of the governor to appoint does not include the power to assign. That is the function of the judiciary (*Ketchum v. Lehner*, 1988).

SECTION 34. JUDICIAL TERM OF OFFICE

The justices of the Supreme Court and judges of all subordinate courts, except Assistant Judges and Judges of Probate, shall hold office for terms of six years except when holding office under an interim appointment. At the end of the initial six year term and at the end of each six year term thereafter, such justice or judge may give notice in the manner provided by law of his desire to continue in office. When such justice or judge gives the required notice, the question of his continuance in office shall be submitted to the General Assembly and he shall continue in office for another term of six years unless a majority of the members of the General Assembly voting on the question vote against his continuing in office.

In the original Pennsylvania Constitution the supreme court justices were to be commissioned for seven years but could be reappointed. This provision for a fixed term was not carried over into the 1777 Vermont Constitution. It was not until Article of Amendment 26 in 1870 that a fixed term for supreme court justices was constitutionally guaranteed, and then for only two years. Attempts had been made earlier to fix their term at a longer period. In 1813 it was proposed that they hold office for life. This suggestion by the fifth Council of Censors was rejected by the convention of 1814. In 1821 the sixth Council of Censors recommended a seven-year term. This was rejected by the convention of 1821. Seven years was again suggested by the council in 1842 and again was rejected by the convention. In 1856 the eleventh Council of Censors recommended that the judges of the supreme court be classified to provide for staggered terms of office and their terms set at six years. This suggestion was rejected by the ninety-person convention of 1857. In 1880 a sweeping amendment was proposed that would have reorganized the courts. Included among its provisions was one that the judges of the supreme court would be appointed for eight years and their terms so staggered that one judge would go out of office every two years. (Another provision called for a supreme court consisting of a chief justice and three associate justices.) This proposed amendment never passed the Senate. In 1920 a ten-year term was proposed. Again this proposal was rejected by the Senate.

In *Wolfe v. Yudichak* (1989) a retired justice joined in the opinion of the court. It was held that a justice can complete work on a case that he heard before retirement. The justice's status was fixed on the date of hearing.

In *Peck v. Douglas* (1987) the court determined that all justices have the same commencement date.

SECTION 35. MANDATORY RETIREMENT

All justices of the Supreme Court and judges of all subordinate courts shall be retired at the end of the calendar year in which they attain seventy years of age or at the end of the term of election during which they attain seventy years of age, as the case may be, and shall be pensioned as provided by law. The chief justice may from time to time appoint retired justices and judges to special assignments as permitted under the rules of the Supreme Court.

This section has no counterpart in the Constitution of 1793. It was added to the constitution through Article of Amendment 46 in 1974. It was immediately challenged by two assistant judges, both over seventy, alleging that this provision violated the equal protection clause of the Fourteenth Amendment to the United States Constitution.

In *Aronstam v. Cashman* (1974) the court rejected this argument. The court noted:

> We have not been shown by the plaintiffs any recognized fundamental personal right that has been violated by the people of Vermont by mandating judicial retirement at seventy years of age. On the other hand, we recognize the legitimate State interest in requiring for members of the judiciary the highest possible standard obtainable by minimizing as far as possible the threat of an obviously disabled judge continuing to preside in full view of the eyes of the public. The processes of disciplinary control by this Court and impeachment have been examined and rejected because of the even greater threat of the intervening loss of public confidence in the courts of Vermont during the course of such proceedings.

The issue has again been brought into litigation through the act of Congress striking all mandatory retirement laws. A supreme court justice arrived at the mandatory age of retirement. He objected to his retirement, claiming that the federal Age Discrimination in Employment Act, at least as far as the mandatory retirement of appointed judges is concerned, takes precedence over Section 35. The district court in *E.E.O.C. v. State of Vermont* (1989) agreed. The opinion was affirmed in 1990 by the Second Circuit Court of Appeals. It was overruled by the United States Supreme Court.

The assignment of retired justices to hear a case in superior court was questioned in *Condosta v. Condosta* (1981). The court quickly disposed of the question, noting that Section 35 of Chapter 2 provides for the assignment of retired justices by the chief justice.

SECTION 36. SUSPENSION AND REMOVAL; IMPLEMENTATION PROCEDURES FOR SECTIONS 32 THROUGH 36

> The justices of the Supreme Court and the judges of all subordinate courts shall hold office during good behavior for the terms for which they are appointed. The Supreme Court in the exercise of its disciplinary power over the judiciary of the state may suspend justices of the Supreme Court and judges of all subordinate courts from the judicial function for such cause and in such manner as may be provided by law.

> The General Assembly may establish procedures for the implementation of the provisions of sections thirty-two through thirty-six.

This section appears for the first time as part of Article of Amendment 46. The court has implemented its disciplinary powers by enacting a judicial code of conduct. The supreme court does have power of suspension from service of a retired justice (*In re Hill*, 1989).

SECTION 37. RULE-MAKING POWER

> The Supreme Court shall make and promulgate rules governing the administration of all courts, and shall make and promulgate rules governing practice and procedure in civil and criminal cases in all courts. Any rule adopted by the Supreme Court may be revised by the General Assembly.

There has been a long history in Vermont of subservience of the judiciary to the legislature in the matter of rules of procedure. The constitution did not grant authority for such rules to either the legislative or judicial branch. The court reform provisions in Article of Amendment 46 attempted to clarify this power. However, although the section seems to grant authority to the supreme court, the last sentence has caused confusion.

It would appear that the committee that proposed this provision was attempting to ensure the passage of the section through the legislature. The section as written and adopted did not settle any power struggle between the legislative and judicial branches. The section has not been judicially reviewed.

SECTION 38. JURY TRIALS

> Trials of issues, proper for the cognizance of a Jury as established by law or by judicial rules adopted by the Supreme Court not inconsistent with law, in the Supreme Court, the Superior Court and other subordinate courts, shall be by Jury, except where parties otherwise agree; and great care ought to be taken to prevent corruption or partiality in the choice and return, or appointment of Juries.

Section 25 of the 1776 Pennsylvania Constitution contained the following: "Trials shall be by jury as heretofore: And it is recommended to the legislature of this state, to provide by law against every corruption or partiality in the choice, return, or appointment of juries." The Windsor Convention in 1777 adopted this language in Section 22. In 1786 the language was revised to read: "Trials of issues, proper for the cognizance of a jury, in the supreme and county courts, shall be by jury, except where parties otherwise agree; and great care ought to be taken to prevent corruption or partiality in the choice and return, or appointment of juries." The 1793 Constitution adopted this language, which remained until Article of Amendment 46 in 1974, which gave us the present language.

The cases that have interpreted this language have, in the main, been discussed under Article 12 of Chapter 1 of the constitution. *Hall v. Armstrong* (1893) at page 424 declares Section 31 (present 38) to have the same effect as Article 12. Neither this section nor Article 12 secured a jury trial in questions raised in equity, admiralty, or probate proceedings (*In re Welch's Will*, 1896).

The leading case on the question of right to trial by jury is *Plimpton v. Town of Somerset* (1860). In that case the legislature had established a new action but damages were to be determined by commissioners and not necessarily by jury. The court declared that the issues to which a jury trial was guaranteed were those which existed at common law or would arise by subsequent legislation. The test was the nature of the controversy between the parties.

After discussing Article 12, the court, in *State v. Peterson* (1869), declared, "In order, therefore, to remove all doubt as to the right of the parties to a trial by a common law jury, and as to the court or courts in which that right is secured and may be enjoyed, section 31 (now 38) of the constitution provides that 'trials of issues proper for the cognizance of the jury, in the supreme and county courts, shall be by jury, except where the parties otherwise agree.'"

In *State v. Hirsch* (1917) the court held that all courts having final jurisdiction must guarantee a trial by jury. But notice of a request for such jury trial may be required (*Muzzy v. Curtis*, 1969).

During a medical malpractice case an affidavit was presented to the court in which it was claimed that a juror was now known to be prejudiced. The trial court refused to determine the truth of the allegations but continued the trial. On appeal the court returned the case for determination of the truth of the allegation. The court held that, if true, the allegations would be sufficient to disqualify the juror because "great care ought to be taken to prevent corruption or partiality in the choice and return, or appointment of juries" (*Isabelle v. Proctor Hospital*, 1971).

SECTION 39. FORMS OF PROSECUTIONS AND INDICTMENTS; FINES

All prosecutions shall commence, *By the authority of the State of Vermont*. All Indictments shall conclude with these words, *against the peace and dignity of the State*. And all fines shall be proportioned to the offences.

The Pennsylvania constitutional provision was adopted verbatim in the Vermont Constitution of 1777, Section 34. By Section 29 of the 1786

Constitution, the present language of Section 39 was adopted. The new language contained the provision relating to fines.

In Vermont prosecutions may be commenced by an indictment of a grand jury or an information filed by a prosecuting officer. In *State v. Bell* (1978) the prosecution was commenced by information which concluded with the words "against the peace and dignity of the State." After conviction the defendant appealed, claiming that the conclusion was a substantive element of the offense and therefore must be proved. The court held on the authority of *State v. Amidon* (1885) that the conclusion "against the peace and dignity of the State" was not substantive as to the crime alleged and therefore need not be proved.

The word "fines" in this section connotes all punishments: fines, imprisonment, forfeiture, or disqualification (*State v. Burlington Drug Company*, 1911).

SECTION 40. EXCESSIVE BAIL PROHIBITED; PRISONERS BAILABLE; IMPRISONMENT FOR DEBT PROHIBITED

> Excessive bail shall not be exacted for bailable offenses. All persons, unless sentenced, or unless committed for offenses punishable by death or life imprisonment when the evidence of guilt is great, shall be bailable by sufficient sureties. Persons committed for offenses punishable by death or life imprisonment, when the evidence of guilt is great, shall not be bailable as a matter of right. No person shall be imprisoned for debt.

The present Section 40 was structured by Article of Amendment 49 in 1982. Vermont does not have any constitutional provision relative to cruel and unusual punishment. The court, in *State v. Burlington Drug Co.* (1911), declared the Eighth Amendment to the United States Constitution not applicable to the state even through the Fourteenth Amendment. That case has since been overruled by *Robinson v. California* (1962).

Bail, if granted, must be forthcoming to warrant the release of a criminal defendant. When there has been a conviction, however, the court has held that even though an appeal was pending, the defendant had to comply strictly with conditions of release pending that appeal. In *In re Comolli* (1906) the attempt to post bail the day following incarceration was too late.

In the matter of bail, the court has held that its purpose is to assure the defendant's presence in court. The legislature saw fit to enact a statute that provided for pretrial preventive detention. In *State v. Pray* (1975) the court held that as the respondent was not in execution of sentence, the action of the trial court in denying bail because the respondent constituted a danger to the public was contrary to Section 40. However, in that same act, the legislature set out other factors that the court could take into consideration in setting bail. All those conditions except the anticipatory test of danger to the public the court held proper in *State v. Mecier* (1978).

Denial of bail for a breach of conditions imposed, however, does not necessarily violate the constitution. In *State v. Brown* (1978) the court commenced its discussion by stating that there is an obvious conflict between Section 40 to assure defendant's appearance and the interest of society in having dangerous persons restrained. It proceeded to affirm the holding in *Pray* that no preventive detention is to be permitted to deny bail, but all other conditions may be imposed when, if breached, bail may be revoked. The court did hold that there must be a hearing to determine the breach of condition. In *State v. Cyr* (1976) it was held that the trial court could not imprison a respondent pending a hearing on revocation of bail or imposition of conditions of release.

Is one held on a governor's warrant entitled to bail? The court has answered this question in the negative. In *In re Iverson* (1977) the court reasoned that detaining a fugitive was only for the rendition to a sister state. "Bail and conditions of release derive from the charge, embodied in the substantive offense, and are determined by the courts of the demanding state."

Imprisonment for debt is constitutionally outlawed in Vermont by the last sentence of Section 40. It was not until the adoption of Article of Amendment 49 in 1982 that imprisonment for debt was declared unconstitutional. Prior to that article of amendment, Section 40 (formerly Section 33 of the 1793 Constitution) commenced with the following language:

> The person of a debtor, where there is not a strong presumption of fraud, shall not be continued in prison after his delivering up and assigning over, bona fide, all his estate, real and personal, in possession, reversion or remainder, for the use of his creditors, in such manner as shall be regulated by law.

In *State v. Carpenter* (1980) the court struck down a statute where a failure to pay a debt (unpaid wages) without a further finding of a "strong presumption of fraud" made such criminal statute unconstitutional as not fully complying with Section 40.

Since the adoption of Article of Amendment 49 the court through a single justice has rendered one opinion (*State v. Lambert*, 1985). In that case the trial court had denied bail for one accused of second degree murder, which carried a maximum penalty of life imprisonment. The denial of bail was based on that fact and a finding that the evidence of guilt was great. The single justice reversed and ordered a hearing to determine whether the respondent would appear for trial if released on bail as authorized by a statute which in part had been declared unconstitutional but which referred to the former Section 40 where only the crimes punishable by death were possibly nonbailable. The justice held that "thus, constitutional provisions prohibit action by the Legislature beyond the limitations imposed, but do not affect statutes whose terms come within those limitations."

The release of Pray and Cyr through the declaration that the purpose of bail was only to ensure the appearance of the defendants at trial led to the note in 2 VT L Rev 217 (1977). The Constitution of 1793 in Section 32 of Chapter 2 had referred to capital offenses. A capital offense was one punishable by death (*State v. Pray,* 1975). The death penalty having been abolished, Pray was allowed bail. The note discusses the possibilities of still denying bail in order to protect the public.

It is obvious that the new language in Article of Amendment 49 referring to life imprisonment was a reflection on the definition of capital offenses. This was the subject of a note in 8 VT L Rev 347 (1983). That note discussed the new restrictions on the right to bail set out in the amended Section 40. There is a continuing pressure to restrict bail further as long as the crime rate increases.

SECTION 41. HABEAS CORPUS

The Writ of Habeas Corpus shall in no case be suspended. It shall be a writ issuable of right; and the General Assembly shall make provision to render it a speedy and effectual remedy in all cases proper therefor.

The purpose of the writ of habeas corpus is to provide a summary proceeding to determine the lawfulness of one's imprisonment or restraint (*In re Turner,* 1918).

This section became part of the constitution by Article of Amendment 12 (1836). The reason for the writ becoming part of the constitution is unclear as it apparently has always been available as part of the law of the state (e.g., *Ex parte Bryant,* 1803). Even the 1814 legislature had passed a statute declaring that habeas corpus "is a writ of right." This statute was declared to concern imprisonment on civil process as well as criminal proces (*Hathaway v. Holmes,* 1828).

Nor was a release on habeas corpus necessarily a bar to a subsequent civil imprisonment (*Eldred v. Wright,* 1830). Could habeas corpus be extended to relieve from imprisonment on *final* civil process? Yes, said the court in *Kellogg ex parte* (1834).

The writ was not available, however, when other remedies could have been used (*In re Hosley,* 1850). There abatement as to one issue and a mandamus as to another issue were the correct actions. Nor would the court, upon habeas corpus, reexamine the proceedings of the magistrate de novo (*In re Powers,* 1853).

In *In re Foot* (1859) the court did not insist upon speedy release as seemingly required by this section.

In *In re Miles* (1880) the petitioner had been brought to Vermont from New York by virtue of a governor's warrant. He claimed that the transportation from New York was illegal. The Vermont Supreme Court held: "The sheriff of Washington County was holding a warrant for the arrest of Miles upon the pending indictment against him. He found Miles within his precinct. He had official authority, and it was his official duty, to make the arrest commanded by said warrant, without regard to the means by which Miles had been brought within his reach and power."

In re Byron (1909) was an action for habeas corpus brought by the next friend (mother) of a four-year-old child (a bastard) held by her putative father. The court ruled that habeas corpus was proper to return the child to the mother, who was presumed to be the proper custodian.

The denial of the writ does not bar another petition to the same court (*In re Turner*, 1918). The court cited with approval that the relator "may renew his application to every court in the kingdom having jurisdiction, until he obtains his liberty."

The court, in *In re Rickert* (1964), reviewed much of the law relative to habeas corpus. The court restated the proposition that the petition should not be held to "the intricacies and pitfalls of strict practice and procedure, or be scrutinized with technical niceties." It also denied this petition on the ground that Rickert's appeal, which was then pending, would present all matters alleged in his petition and that a writ of habeas corpus was not to be used as a substitute for an appeal. It was also held that the statutes providing postconviction relief are not in derogation of this section (*Shequin v. Smith*, 1971).

Qualifications of Freemen

SECTION 42. FREEMAN'S QUALIFICATIONS AND OATH

Every person of the full age of eighteen years who is a citizen of the United States, having resided in this State for the period established by the General Assembly and who is of a quiet and peaceable behavior, and will take the following oath or affirmation, shall be entitled to all the privileges of a freeman of this state:

You solemnly swear (or affirm) that whenever you give your vote or suffrage, touching any matter that concerns the State of Vermont, you will do it so as in your conscience you shall judge will most conduce to the best good of the same, as established by the Constitution, without fear or favor of any person.

The substance of this section can be found in Section 6 of the Constitution of 1777, in which the age limit was set at twenty-one years and, of course, applied only to men. The resident also had to take the oath prescribed in Section 42. There was a residency requirement of one year before the election of representatives. It became Section 21 of the 1793 Constitution.

Article of Amendment 1 (1828) gave the privileges of a freeman only to those already freemen, to natural born citizens of Vermont or some other state, or to those naturalized "agreeably to the acts of Congress." In 1924, by Article of Amendment 40, "man" was changed to "person" to allow universal suffrage of all citizens twenty-one years of age and to conform to the Nineteenth Amendment to the United States Constitution. Article of Amendment 1 was incorporated into this article of amendment. In 1974, by Article 47, the age was reduced to eighteen to conform to Amendment 26 to the U.S. Constitution.

There has been no litigation specifically concerning this section. The attorney general, however, has issued opinions based on the qualifications of freemen. If a foreigner has lived in Vermont the requisite number of years, he is eligible to vote immediately upon being naturalized (Opinion of the Attorney General, 1968–70). That same report declares that persons living on federal property within the state may vote if otherwise qualified. The attorney general has also stated that the freeman's oath is the only oath necessary to take to be qualified to vote in Vermont.

Elections—Officers—Terms of Office

SECTION 43. BIENNIAL ELECTIONS

> The Governor, Lieutenant-Governor, Treasurer, Secretary of State, Auditor of Accounts, Senators, Town Representatives, Assistant Judges of the County Court, Sheriffs, High Bailiffs, State's Attorneys, Judges of Probate and Justices of the Peace, shall be elected biennially on the first Tuesday next after the first Monday of November, beginning in A.D. 1914.

Under the Vermont Constitution of 1777 all statewide officials were to serve one-year terms, and the constitutions of 1786 and 1793 continued the annual elections.

By Article of Amendment 5 (1836) a Senate was established, and the senators were to be elected annually. Sheriffs, assistant judges of the counties, high bailiffs, state's attorneys, and probate judges, when made constitutional officers by articles of amendment 14, 15, 16, 17, and 18 (1850), were to be elected annually (Article of Amendment 20,1850). These terms became biennial through Article of Amendment 24. By Article of Amendment 28 (1883) the secretary of state and the auditor of accounts were made constitutional officers, and their terms were fixed at two years.

By Article of Amendment 46 of this constitution, four-year terms were designated for assistant judges, sheriffs, state's attorneys, judges of probate, and justices of the peace.

The state's attorney of Windsor County refused to prosecute a case. The attorney general thereupon commenced prosecution. The state's attorney attempted to enjoin the prosecution by the attorney general, claiming, *inter alia,* that he was a constitutional officer and the attorney general was not and therefore his powers were constitutional functions and took precedence over the attorney general's. The court pointed out that the only constitutional provision relating to state's attorneys related to the date of election and the term for which they serve. Their functions, the court continued, are determined by the legislature, and the legislature has given the state's attorneys and the attorney general equal power to initiate criminal prosecutions. The injunction was denied (*State's Attorney v. Attorney General,* 1979).

SECTION 44. ELECTION OF REPRESENTATIVES AND SENATORS

> Senators and Representatives shall be elected to office at a general election to be held biennially on the first Tuesday next after the first Monday of November, A.D. 1974.

The election of senators and representatives had been on the first Tuesday of September (representatives: Constitution of 1777, Section 8; Constitution of 1786, Section 8; Constitution of 1793, Section 8; senators: through Article of Amendment 5 [1836], biennially on the first Tuesday after the first Monday in September, Article of Amendment 24, 1870). The date was changed to the first Tuesday after the first Monday in November (Article of Amendment 30, 1913), which was confirmed in Article of Amendment 48 (1974). This conformed to the federal election. It made elections cost effective. There has been no litigation on this section.

SECTION 45. MANNER OF ELECTION

> The manner of election, certification, and filling of vacancies in office of Senators and Representatives shall be as established by law.

This section was finally established in its present form by Article of Amendment 48 (1974). The phrase "established by law" replaced the phrase "in the manner prescribed by the Constitution of the State" found in Article of Amendment 24. The election of senators was set forth in Article of Amendment 5 (1830) and that of representatives in Section 8 of the 1793 Constitution. The state election law is set out in Title 17 of the Vermont Statutes Annotated. No litigation has resulted from this section.

SECTION 46. TERMS OF SENATORS AND REPRESENTATIVES

The term of office of Senators and Representatives shall be two years, commencing on the first Wednesday next after the first Monday of January following their election.

The terms of the senators and representatives had been one year until Article of Amendment 24 (1870), which extended the term to two years. No litigation has resulted through this section.

SECTION 47. ELECTION OF GOVERNOR, LIEUTENANT-GOVERNOR, AND TREASURER

The freemen of each town shall, on the day of election for choosing Representatives to attend the General Assembly, bring in their votes for Governor, with his name fairly written, to the Constable, who shall seal them up, and write on them, *Votes for Governor*, and deliver them to the Representatives chosen to attend the General Assembly; and at the opening of the General Assembly, there shall be a committee appointed out of the Senate and House of Representatives, who, after being duly sworn to the faithful discharge of their trust, shall proceed to receive, sort, and count the votes for Governor, and declare the person who has the major part of the votes, to be Governor for the two years ensuing. The Lieutenant-Governor and the Treasurer shall be chosen in the manner above directed.

The votes for Governor, Lieutenant-Governor, and Treasurer, of the State, shall be sorted and counted, and the result declared, by a committee appointed by the Senate and House of Representatives.

If, at any time, there shall be no election, by the freemen, of Governor, Lieutenant-Governor, or Treasurer, of the State, the Senate and House of Representatives shall by a joint ballot, elect to fill the office, not filled by the freemen as aforesaid, one of the three candidates for such office (if there be so many) for whom the greatest number of votes shall have been returned.

The section is substantially as it was designed in Section 17 of Chapter 2 of the 1793 Constitution. Of course, the Governor's Council was dropped in 1836, and by Article of Amendment 9 (1836) the present language was substantially adopted.

In *Temple v. Mead* (1832) the constable of Rutland refused to accept the vote of the plaintiff because the names of the officers for whom he was voting were printed on the paper offered. The court held that printing was equated to "fairly written." So the term "fairly written" does not mean that the only votes counted need be in pen and ink. This case gives us the constitutional basis for the present-day printed ballots.

SECTION 48. ELECTION OF SECRETARY OF STATE AND AUDITOR OF ACCOUNTS

The Secretary of State and the Auditor of Accounts shall be elected by the freemen of the State upon the same ticket with the Governor, Lieutenant-Governor and Treasurer; and the Legislature shall carry this provision into effect by appropriate legislation.

These two officials were initially appointed. By Article of Amendment 28 (1883) their election by the people was guaranteed by the constitution. There has been no litigation interpreting this section.

SECTION 49. TERM OF GOVERNOR, LIEUTENANT-GOVERNOR, AND TREASURER

The term of office of the Governor, Lieutenant-Governor and Treasurer of the State, respectively, shall commence when they shall be chosen and qualified, and shall continue for the term of two years, or until their successors shall be chosen and qualified, or to the adjournment of the session of the Legislature at which, by the Constitution and laws, their successors are required to be chosen, and not after such adjournment.

This section was added in 1850 by Article of Amendment 21. That amendment called for a 1 year term. By Article of Amendment 24, section 3 (1870) the term was lengthened to 2 years. There has been no litigation interpreting this section.

SECTION 50. FREEMEN TO ELECT ASSISTANT JUDGES, SHERIFFS, AND STATE'S ATTORNEYS

The Assistant Judges shall be elected by the freemen of their respective districts as established by law. Their judicial functions shall be established by law. Their term of office shall be four years and shall commence on the first day of February next after their election.

Sheriffs shall be elected by the freemen of their respective districts as established by law. Their term of office shall be four years and shall commence on the first day of February next after their election.

State's Attorneys shall be elected by the freemen of their respective districts as established by law. Their term of office shall be four years and shall commence on the first day of February next after their election.

These officials were appointed for one-year terms by the legislature (Section 9, Constitution of 1793). By Article of Amendment 50 (1850) their election was guaranteed by the freemen of their respective counties. Their election for two-year terms was set out in Article of Amendment 30 (1913), and a four-year term was established by Article of Amendment 46 (1974). The change from counties to districts was to conform to the new provisions for senators and representatives.

This section appears to be somewhat in conflict with Section 43. It is, however, an extension of that section, and its provisions, when in conflict, would be paramount, since they were adopted later in time.

As the discussion of Section 43 indicates, the fact that state's attorneys are mentioned in the constitution did not make them superior to the attorney general, an office not appearing in the constitution (*State's Attorney v. Attorney General*, 1979).

A prosecution was commenced by a special prosecutor appointed by the governor in accordance with a legislative act (*In re Snell*, 1885). The defendant brought a habeas corpus claiming, *inter alia*, that the act was in conflict with this section of the constitution establishing the election of state's attorneys by the freemen of their counties. The court stated that the legislature has power to provide for the commencement of prosecutions by informing officers not elected by the people".

SECTION 51. FREEMEN TO ELECT JUDGES OF PROBATE

> Judges of Probate shall be elected by the freemen of their respective districts as established by law. The General Assembly may establish by law qualifications for the election to and holding of such office. Their term of office shall be four years and shall commence on the first day of February next after their election.

By Section 9 of the Constitution of 1793 the probate judges were to be elected by the legislature for a term of one year. By Article of Amendment 17 (1850) their election was to be by the freemen of their respective probate districts. By Article of Amendment 46 (1974) their terms were extended to four years.

Prior to this amendment, there were no qualifications necessary to become a judge of probate. The addition of the language granting power to the legislature to establish qualifications has not resulted in a change. About half of the judges of probate are attorneys; the rest are not.

This section appears to be somewhat in conflict with Section 43. It is, however, an extension of that section, and its provisions, when in conflict, would be paramount, since they were adopted later in time. There is no litigation interpreting this section.

SECTION 52. FREEMEN TO ELECT JUSTICES OF THE PEACE; APPORTIONMENT

Justices of the Peace shall be elected by the freemen of their respective towns; and towns having less than one thousand inhabitants may elect any number of Justices of the Peace not exceeding five; towns having one thousand and less than two thousand inhabitants, may election seven; towns having two thousand and less than three thousand inhabitants, may elect ten; towns having three thousand and less than five thousand inhabitants, may elect twelve; and towns having five thousand, or more, inhabitants, may elect fifteen Justices of the Peace. Justices of the Peace shall not exercise judicial powers, except that they may serve as magistrates when so commissioned by the Supreme Court.

The justices of the peace were elected annually by the legislature by Section 9 of the 1793 Constitution. By Article of Amendment 18 (1850) the number of justices by population was established. These numbers continue to this day. The last sentence of this section was added by Article of Amendment 46 (1974).

The section has not been the subject of litigation, but the attorney general has rendered opinions relative to the apportionment of justices of the peace (Opinion of the Attorney General, 1950–52). The attorney general has also stated that the governor could not appoint extra justices when a town did not elect the maximum number authorized because there was no vacancy (Opinion of the Attorney General, 1960–62).

SECTION 53. ELECTION OF ASSISTANT JUDGES, SHERIFFS, STATE'S ATTORNEYS, JUDGES OF PROBATE, AND JUSTICES OF THE PEACE

The manner and certification of election and filling of vacancies in the offices of Assistant Judges, Sheriffs, State's Attorneys, Judges of Probate and Justices of the Peace shall be as established by law.

These offices were first made elected by freemen rather than the legislature in Article of Amendment 5 (1836). Their election was to be as the senators. Their election was then to be formally determined by the legislature. These officials were then to be given commissions for their terms by the governor. The simple language of this section is as set out in Article of Amendment 46 (1974). The section has not been litigated.

SECTION 54. INCOMPATIBLE OFFICES

> No person in this State shall be capable of holding or exercising more than one of the following offices at the same time: Governor, Lieutenant-Governor, Justice of the Supreme Court, Treasurer of the State, member of the Senate, member of the House of Representatives, Surveyor-General, or Sheriff. Nor shall any person holding any office of profit or trust under the authority of Congress, other than a member of the commissioned or enlisted personnel in the reserve components of the armed forces of the United States while not on extended active duty, be eligible to any appointment in the Legislature, or to any executive or judiciary office under this State.

The substance of this section did not appear in the 1777 Constitution. In Article of Amendment 42 (1954) provision was made to exempt "a member of the commissioned or enlisted personnel in the reserve components of the armed forces of the United States while not on extended active duty." This exemption was included because many veterans of World War II continued their commitment to the United States by joining the reserves or national guard.

In Section 43 of the 1786 Constitution, the governor, lieutenant-governor, judge of the supreme court, treasurer of the state, member of the council, member of the general assembly, surveyor general, or sheriff were prohibited from holding two of these offices at the same time. In the Constitution of 1793 was added the provision: "Nor shall any person holding any office of profit or trust under the authority of Congress be eligible to any appointment in the Legislature, or of holding any executive or judiciary office under this state."

Should the offices of justice of the peace and postmaster be considered incompatible offices? In 1842, in *McGregor v. Balch*, the court held that the office of postmaster was an office of both profit and trust under the authority of Congress. It also held that justice of the peace was a judiciary office under the state. Therefore the two offices could not be held by the same person at the same time.

In *State ex rel v. Edwards* (1925) the postmistress was elected to the school board of the town of Walden. When aware that the offices might be incompatible, she resigned her position as school director. The selectmen declared a vacancy and appointed Edwards. The former school commissioner claimed that no successor had been elected and so no vacancy had occurred. The court agreed, holding that the elected school director could not qualify for the office unless she resigned as postmistress. Failing that, there was no valid election, and the former school director remained in office.

In *State v. Levy* (1943) it was determined that city grand juror was a judiciary office of the state. The court refused to determine whether a referee in bankruptcy held an office of profit or trust under Congress, holding that even if the city grand juror was not qualified to hold office, he was an officer de facto and his acts as respects a third person are valid.

However, postmaster was no longer held to be an office of profit or trust under the authority of Congress because of the change in the law as to postmasters (*Baker v. Hazen*, 1975). The court held that changes in the Postal Reorganization Act of 1971 removed the position from the authority of Congress. The court concluded as follows: "The constitutional provision represents a denial of a right to a citizen. If it cannot be clearly demonstrated that he falls within its proscription, or equally plainly shown that he is in violation of its purpose, he is entitled to be held free of its prohibition."

The question was asked of the attorney general as to whether one person could act as secretary of the Vermont Senate and also as a representative for a congressional office. The attorney general replied that the secretary of the Senate was not a member of the legislature and therefore, regardless of whether representative for a congressional office was an office of profit and trust under Congress, the secretary of the Senate would not have to resign that position (Opinion of the Attorney General, 1962).

When asked whether a person who was a member of the board of social welfare could accept the appointment as federal housing administrator for Vermont, clearly an office of profit and trust under Congress, and remain on the board, the attorney general answered in the negative. He reasoned that the social welfare board's duties were in part judicial and in part executive, and therefore continued membership would violate Section 54.

The following issues relative to Section 54 are among those that have been the subject of opinions by the attorney general: School director and postmaster or collector of internal revenue are incompatible (Opinion of the Attorney General, 1940). One may run for representative and senator at the same time but must renounce one (Opinion of the Attorney General, 1966). Simultaneously holding the offices of federal customs inspector and member of the board of trustees of the Vermont State Colleges is violative of Section 54 (Opinion of the Attorney General, 1964). Member of the International Joint Commission is incompatible with chairman of the Board of Water Resources of the State of Vermont (Opinion of the Attorney General, 1970).

SECTION 55. FREEDOM OF ELECTIONS; BRIBERY

All elections, whether by the people or the Legislature, shall be free and voluntary: and any elector who shall receive any gift or reward for his vote, in meat, drink, moneys or otherwise, shall forfeit his right to elect at that time, and suffer such other penalty as the law shall direct; and any person who shall directly or indirectly give,

> promise, or bestow, any such rewards to be elected, shall thereby be rendered incapable to serve for the ensuing year, and be subject to such further punishment as the Legislature shall direct.

The Constitution of 1777 in Section 29 adopted Section 32 of the Pennsylvania Constitution almost verbatim. This provision has not been judicially interpreted.

Oath of Allegiance—Oath of Office

SECTION 56. OATHS OF ALLEGIANCE AND OFFICE

Every officer, whether judicial, executive or military, in authority under this State, before he enters upon the execution of his office, shall take and subscribe the following oath or affirmation of allegiance to this State, (unless he shall produce evidence that he has before taken the same) and also the following oath or affirmation of office, except military officers and such as shall be exempted by the Legislature.

The oath or affirmation of allegiance

You———do solemnly swear (or affirm) that you will be true and faithful to the State of Vermont; and that you will not, directly or indirectly, do any act or thing injurious to the constitution or government thereof as established by convention. (If an oath) *So help you God.* (If an affirmation) *under the pains and penalties of perjury.*

The oath or affirmation of office

You———do solemnly swear (or affirm) that you will faithfully execute the office of———for the———of———; and will therein do equal right and justice to all men, to the best of your judgment and abilities, according to law. (If an oath) *So held you God.* (If an affirmation) *under the pains and penalties of perjury.*

The Vermont Constitution of 1777 contained substantially the same oaths in Section 36 as did the Pennsylvania Constitution of 1776 in its Section 40. In 1786 the convention added "(unless he shall produce evidence that he has before taken the same)" in Section 26. The exception "except . . . such as shall be exempted by the Legislature" was also added. The military also had to take the oath of office as well as the oath of allegiance. That requirement was deleted from the 1793 Constitution. The present Section 56 has remained unchanged since 1793.

A constable of a town need not take the oath set out in this section as he is not an "officer in authority under this State" (*Bixby v. Roscoe,* 1911), nor is it necessary for a town lister to take the constitutional oath (*Rowell v. Horton,* 1886). A special prosecutor was appointed by the governor to try a particular case. The defendant in *Petition of Dusablon* (1967) contended that there was no showing in the record that the special counsel ever received and subscribed to the oath contained in this section. The court held that there was a presumption that the authority to act was properly conferred. The court further concluded that the prosecutor was a de facto officer, and that would be sufficient to sustain the conviction. Acts of an officer de facto are valid so far as they concern the public, of the rights of third persons, as if the officer was de jure. (*Lyndon v. Miller,* 1863). However, if the action is against the office holder, the ruling would be different (*Courser v. Powers,* 1861, and *Houston v. Russell,* 1879).

The children of an elected probate judge advised the governor that their father, due to his physical and mental condition, was unable to perform the duties of his office. The attorney general, in response to a request of the governor for an opinion as to the office of the probate judge under these circumstances, replied that a vacancy existed, as the elected official failed to take the oath required under this section (Opinion of the Attorney General, 1962).

Impeachments

SECTION 57. HOUSE MAY ORDER IMPEACHMENTS

The House of Representatives shall have the power to order impeachments, which shall in all cases be by a vote of two-thirds of its members.

The power to order impeachments was originally vested in the Council of Censors, under the Vermont Constitution of 1777 (Section 46), and the Vermont constitutions of 1786 (Section 40) and 1793 (Section 43) continued this practice. It was not until the abolition of the Council of Censors in 1870 (Article of Amendment 25) that the power was transferred to the House of Representatives, where it resides today.

In contrast to the federal constitution, Section 57 contains no specifications or basis for determining impeachments. There has been no litigation interpreting this section.

SECTION 58. LIABILITY TO IMPEACHMENT; TRIAL BY SENATE; JUDGMENT

Every officer of State, whether judicial or executive, shall be liable to be impeached by the House of Representatives, either when in office or after his resignation or removal for maladministration.

> The Senate shall have the sole power of trying and deciding upon all impeachments. When sitting for that purpose, they shall be on oath, or affirmation, and no person shall be convicted, without the concurrence of two-thirds of the members present. Judgment in cases of impeachment shall not extend further than to removal from office and disqualification to hold or enjoy any office of honor, or profit, or trust, under this State. But the person convicted shall, nevertheless, be liable and subject to indictment, trial, judgment, and punishment, according to law.

The body originally designated to try impeachments was the governor or lieutenant-governor and council (Constitution of 1777, Section 20). With the advent of the Senate in 1836, the power to try impeachments was transferred to the Senate by Article of Amendment 7. The governor's power was specifically excised by Article of Amendment 8 (1836).

A justice of the peace was elected to that office in October 1799. His term was to commence as of December 1, 1799, and terminate one year later. After his term expired it was alleged in a criminal indictment that he had antedated a writ of execution to November 29, 1800. In *State v. Campbell* (1802) the court held that "when it is said 'no trial or impeachment shall be a bar to a prosecution at law,' *civil prosecutions* are alone intended". The court therefore dismissed the indictment.

The sheriff of Washington County was acquitted of charges of impeachment by the Vermont Senate. He sued the state of Vermont for legal expenses incurred in the impeachment proceedings. The court held, in *Mayo v. State* (1980), that the statute that defines the obligation of the state to defend its employees has no application to impeachment proceedings. The statute permits recovery in any *action* or *suit*, and impeachment is at most quasi-judicial in nature. An action or suit connotes a demand in a court of justice or in some tribunal "as a condition precedent to giving a court jurisdiction of the subject matter."

Militia

SECTION 59. MILITIA

The inhabitants of this State shall be trained and armed for its defense, under such regulations, restrictions, and exceptions, as Congress, agreeably to the Constitution of the United States, and the Legislature of this State, shall direct.

The present language of this section was adopted in Article of Amendment 43 (1954). This section has not been judicially reviewed.

General Provisions

SECTION 60. LEGISLATURE RESTRICTED

> No person ought in any case, or in any time, to be declared guilty of treason or felony, by the Legislature, nor to have his sentence upon conviction for felony commuted, remitted or mitigated by the Legislature.

This section first appeared as Section 17 of the Constitution of 1786. The present language was adopted through Article of Amendment 32 (1913). That same amendment removed the prohibition against pardoning for murder exercised by the governor.

Rebideau v. Moeykens (1973) was an appeal from a denial of a petition for post-conviction relief. Rebideau had been convicted of murder in the first degree and sentenced to life imprisonment in the custody of the commissioner of corrections. He claimed that when the legislature deleted "in the state's prison" as the place of confinement to the custody of the commissioner of corrections, it had violated Section 56 (now Section 60) of the Vermont Constitution. The court simply said that "Chapter II, Section 56, of the Vermont Constitution bars the Legislature from commuting, remitting, or mitigating the sentences of individual felons; it does not affect the Legislature's powers to enact laws of general jurisdiction."

SECTION 61. OFFICES OF PROFIT; COMPENSATION; ILLEGAL FEES

As every freeman, to preserve his independence (if without a sufficient estate) ought to have some profession, calling, trade, or farm, whereby he may honestly subsist, there can be no necessity for, nor use in, establishing offices of profit, the usual effect of which are dependence and servility, unbecoming freemen, in the possessors or expectants, and faction, contention, and disorder, among the people. But if any man is called into public service, to the prejudice of his private affairs, he has a right to a reasonable compensation; and whenever an office through increase of fees or otherwise, becomes so profitable as to occasion many to apply for it, the profit ought to be lessened by the Legislature. And if any officer shall wittingly and willfully take greater fees than the law allows him, it shall ever after disqualify him from holding any office in this State, until he shall be restored by act of legislation.

This section, except for the last sentence, was Section 36 of the Pennsylvania Constitution of 1776. It became Section 33 of the Vermont Constitution of 1777. The last sentence would be found in the last clause of Section 26 of the Pennsylvania Constitution and the last clause of the 1777 Constitution. The sections were combined in Section 22 of the Constitution of 1786, except for the provision for reinstatement, which was added to Section 25 of the Constitution of 1793. That section is now Section 61.

In *Welch v. Seery* (1980), Welch requested that Seery, town clerk of Hartford, disclose all fees accrued to her as town clerk. Seery refused. Action was brought to force such disclosure. The town clerk of Hartford received, for her services, a salary. She also received fees defined as "earnings due for official services, aside from salaries or per diem compensation." The plaintiff (Welch) complained, *inter alia*, that Seery's refusal to disclose her fees violated this section. The court quickly disposed of this claim, saying:

> The remedy envisioned by this section is clear. The Legislature established the Office of Town Clerk, sets its fees, and has the power to modify or abolish the powers or fees of the office. Moreover, since the fees are established by statute, unless the town clerk was exacting fees greater than permitted, which is not claimed to be the case here, Section 61 is inapposite.

The court suggested that the remedy was popular election.

SECTION 62. RECORD OF DEEDS

All deeds and conveyances of land shall be recorded in the Town Clerk's office in their respective towns; and, for want thereof, in the County Clerk's office in the same county.

Section 31 of the Constitution of 1777 provided that "all deeds and conveyances of land shall be recorded in the Town Clerk's office, in their respective towns." In the Constitution of 1786 the present language of this section was adopted (Section 32). There are areas in Vermont not encompassed within a town called Gores. Their deeds are recorded in the County Clerk's office.

This section has been held to refer to conveyances of land between living persons and not to wills-conveyed land as devises (*Smith v. Perry*, 1854).

SECTION 63. ENTAILS

The Legislature shall regulate entails in such manner as to prevent perpetuities.

This rule against perpetuities was first adopted from Section 37 of the Pennsylvania Constitution of 1776 through Section 34 of the 1777 Constitution. Its present language was written in Section 33 of the Constitution of 1786.

This section prohibited real property from being conveyed by one instrument for eternity. It did not, however, abolish the right of individuals to restrict the disposition of real property for a period of time subject to designation by the legislature (fee tail). In *Giddings v. Smith* (1843) property was devised to "Elizabeth Harris, and the lawful heirs of her body." Elizabeth Harris and her husband conveyed the property by deed. The children of Elizabeth as heirs of her body sued to eject the subsequent grantee from the property. The court held that the will established a fee tail and that the legislature had never acted to abolish such estates. Therefore, Elizabeth Harris only received, by will, a life estate and could not convey to anyone a fee. The fee rested in the hands of her children. Fee tail has since been abolished by the legislature (27 VSA Sec. 1).

SECTION 64. PUNISHMENT AT HARD LABOR

To deter more effectually from the commission of crimes, by continued visible punishments of long duration, and to make sanguinary punishment less necessary, means ought to be provided for punishing by hard labor, those who shall be convicted of crimes not capital, whereby the criminal shall be employed for the benefit of the public, or for the reparation of injuries done to private persons: and all persons at proper times ought to be permitted to see them at their labor.

This section is derived from Section 39 of the Pennsylvania Constitution of 1776. The present language of the section was adopted in Section 34 of the Constitution of 1786 and carried through the 1793 Constitution as Section 37.

When the only maximum security prison in Vermont was closed and an agreement reached with the federal government placing some of the prisoners in the federal system, such action was challenged in *Battick v. Stoneman* (1976). The federal district court held that such action did not violate this section. The court said that this section is not mandatory.

SECTION 65. SUICIDE'S ESTATE

The estates of such persons as may destroy their own lives shall not, for that offence, be forfeited, but shall descend or ascend in the same manner as if such persons had died in a natural way. Nor shall any article which shall accidentally occasion the death of any person, be deemed a deodand, or in any wise forfeited, on account of such misfortune.

This section appeared for the first time as Section 35 of the Constitution of 1786 and continued as Section 38 of the Constitution of 1793. The section modified the English law which at that time made the estates of suicides forfeited to the state; nor should a personal chattel which caused death be forfeited (deodand). It has not been the subject of any litigation.

SECTION 66. CITIZENSHIP

Every person of good character, who comes to settle in this State, having first taken an oath or affirmation of allegiance to the same, may purchase, or by other just means acquire, hold and transfer land, or other real estate; and after one year's residence shall be deemed a free denizen thereof, and entitled to all the rights of a natural born subject of this state, except the privileges of a freeman, the right to which is herein elsewhere determined, and except also that he shall not be capable of being elected Governor, Treasurer or Representative in Assembly, until after two years residence, nor be eligible to the office of Governor or Lieutenant-Governor until he shall have resided in this State as required by Section 23 of this Constitution.

Part of this section was taken from the 1777 Constitution of Pennsylvania, Section 42, and the Constitution of 1777, Section 38. The only prohibition was a two-years' residence to be elected a representative. The reference was not to "every person" but to "every foreigner." Section 36 of the Constitution of 1786 changed "foreigner" to "person" and extended the two-year residence requirement to the governor, lieutenant-governor, treasurer, or councillor. The Constitution of 1793 in Section 39 carried on the language of the 1786 Constitution.

The words "except the privileges of a freeman, the right to which is herein elsewhere determined . . . nor be eligible to the office of Governor or Lieutenant-Governor until he shall have resided in this State as required by Section 23 of this Constitution" were inserted by the supreme court in 1913 under authority to revise Chapter 2 contained in Article of Amendment 36 (1913). There is no record of the reason for this insertion.

In *Bondi v. MacKay* (1913) the court was faced with determining what constituted residence in the state. Bondi was a bona fide resident of Barre and had been for fourteen years. He did not own real estate. He was born in Italy but was never naturalized. He desired a resident hunting license, which would cost seventy-five cents. The town clerk refused to issue that license but offered a nonresident license at ten dollars and fifty cents. The court held that residence for purposes of this section can only be for a natural or naturalized person. The conclusion was that the failure of Bondi to be naturalized or to take the oath or affirmation required by this section constituted him a nonresident for the purpose of licensing to hunt.

SECTION 67. HUNTING, FOWLING, AND FISHING

> The inhabitants of this State shall have liberty in seasonable times to hunt and fowl on the lands they hold, and on other lands not enclosed, and in like manner to fish in all boatable and other waters (not private property) under proper regulations, to be hereafter made and provided by the general assembly.

This section was substantively adopted in the Constitution of 1793. It invests the legislature with broad powers to regulate the wildlife of the state, including regulating hunting and fishing (*State v. Racine*, 1974).

In *Cabot v. Thomas* (1986) the court was faced with the question of hunting and fishing on lands enclosed by posting at low water mark where persons were in a boat inland of the low water mark post. The court pointed out the distinction between hunting and fishing in Section 67. Hunting was only allowed on non-owned land when the land was not enclosed. Here, the court held that the lands were enclosed, so no hunting would be allowed. In the matter of fishing, however, the same court came to a different conclusion, holding that boatability was the key.

Before the state of Vermont revoked its poll tax provision, the attorney general was asked whether a bill that made the failure to pay a poll tax equivalent to nonresidency, therefore making it necessary for a person who had not paid the tax to obtain a nonresident fish and game license, was constitutional. He replied that such an act would be unconstitutional as it was an attempt to tie a revenue measure to the right to hunt and fish. In his opinion the General Assembly could only make regulations in regard to the rights to hunt and fish (Opinion of the Attorney General, 1962).

In *State v. Norton* (1873) the issue was whether a legislative prohibition on the taking of deer for a period of ten years violated this section. The court held that the act did not, saying that the right was reserved to the General Assembly "to determine what were seasonable times in which to hunt and fowl, and having exercised this right, the court will not assume (certainly in the absence of proof) that it has been exercised in an unconstitutional manner."

The legislature delegated to the Fish and Game Commission the power to grant increased protection to trout and black bear. In *Elliott v. Fish and Game Commission* (1951) the petitioners claimed that this was an unconstitutional delegation of power, arguing that the constitution in Section 63 (now Section 67) granted power to the legislature and not to the commission. The court held that such delegation was constitutional, saying further that legislatures must be able to delegate to the commission or the commissioner power to make regulations as long as the regulations complied with constitutional requirements.

The court has held that the word "inhabitants" as used in this section is not synonymous with "residents." The inhabitants of this state who are secured rights in game by Chapter II, section 67 are the same as "'the people of this state' who are given the power to regulate those rights by Chapter I, Article 5; and these last are the people who act 'by their legal representatives'; a designation which plainly points to the native-born and naturalized inhabitants of the State—the citizen body from which the electorate is taken" (*Bondi v. MacKay*, 1913).

When questioned as to whether the Fish and Game Board has the power to prohibit the trapping of bear, the attorney general answered yes (Opinion of the Attorney General, 1968). He cited this section as guaranteeing the right to hunt and the power of the legislature to regulate. He further cited statutes authorizing the board to amend, revise, revoke, or supersede any regulations established by the General Assembly.

In *Zanetta v. Bolles* (1907) the defendant, accused of killing plaintiff's dog, which was, with other dogs, worrying a deer on his property during the closed season, claimed in defense that once the deer came within his property, it was his and he had a right to protect it, even to killing a dog. Not so, said the court:

> The wild game in the State belongs to the people of the State in their collective and sovereign capacity, and not in their individual and private capacity, except so far as private ownership may be acquired therein under the Constitution, subject to such proper regulations as the Legislature may make.

The court concluded that as the defendant had no right to hunt deer in closed season, he had no property in the deer, so he had no right to kill the dog.

Even though the court found some discrimination between residents and nonresidents, the discrimination was, in effect, too slight to make statutes unconstitutional.

> There is a clear discrimination in the law, as has been shown, in favor of non-residents in respect to having the carcass exposed to view, labelling, etc. But we think that a

non-resident person, having paid for and obtained a license and having killed a deer under his license, acquires such a property in the body of the animal that it may be removed from the State without its being open to view, tagged, labelled, etc. In this respect the act is not unconstitutional (*State v. Niles*, 1906).

Boatable waters have been held as waters that are of "common passage" as highways (*New England Trout &s Salmon Club v. Mather*, 1895). In a dissenting opinion it was said that "boatable" meant boatable and not navigable. The case further holds that access to those waters cannot be had over privately owned land. (The attorney general in an opinion suggested that a highway be laid out to the body of water so enclosed.)

Boatable water was one of the issues raised in *Hazen v. Perkins* (1918). The court found, as a matter of law, that Lake Morey was boatable and thus subject to regulation by the state. The facts of the size of the lake, its use, and the use of the shoreline were all presented through an appointed special master and were found sufficient to constitute the lake boatable as a matter of law.

Does spring flooded land constitute boatable waters? The attorney general considers the question to be one of fact. In his opinion, such shallow water flooding of private property in the spring would not be boatable (Opinion of the Attorney General, 1972).

The water supply for the city of Montpelier comes from Berlin Pond, a boatable body of water. The State Board of Health promulgated an order prohibiting boating on Berlin Pond. Defendant claimed constitutional protection. The court held that the defendant has privileges, but these are subject to the police power of the state to protect the health and safety of its citizens (*State v. Quattropani*, 1926).

What rights do landowners have when they enclose their property? In the case of streams, not boatable, adjoining owners have the right to fish and to keep trespassers off their land. They cannot, however, obstruct the passage of fish which they do not take. They do not own the flowing water but can only use it in a reasonable manner. They must leave it in such condition that landowners above and below may enjoy it equally (*State v. Haskell*, 1911).

The *Theriault* case (*State v. Theriault*, 1898) arose from a defense of unconstitutionality of an act which authorized the fish and game commissioners, when they stocked a stream with fish, to prohibit fishing in the stream or parts of it for a period of years. Theriault was a riparian owner who was prohibited from fishing on his property through an order of the fish and game commissioners who had stocked the stream with fish. The court held that such action was not unconstitutional for the reasons quoted in the *Haskell case*.

SECTION 68. LAWS TO ENCOURAGE VIRTUE AND PREVENT VICE; SCHOOLS; RELIGIOUS ACTIVITIES

> Laws for the encouragement of virtue and prevention of vice and immorality, ought to be constantly kept in force, and duly executed; and a competent number of schools ought to be maintained in each town unless the General Assembly permits other provisions for the convenient instruction of youth. All religious societies, or bodies of men that may be united or incorporated for the advancement of religion and learning, or for other pious and charitable purposes, shall be encouraged and protected in the enjoyment of the privileges, immunities, and estates, which they in justice ought to enjoy, under such regulations as the General Assembly of this State shall direct.

Sections 40 and 41 of the Constitution of 1777, combined in Section 38 of the Constitution of 1786 and carried forward as Section 41 of the Constitution of 1793, called for the maintenance of "one grammar school in each county." The Constitution of 1777 also called for "one university in this State," the grammar schools and university to be "established by direction of the General Assembly." Article of Amendment 41 (1954) included a provision for schools to be maintained by towns jointly with the consent of the legislature. The present language was adopted by Article of Amendment 44 (1964), which changed that provision with the following language "unless the general assembly permits other provisions for the convenient instruction of youth."

The new language was almost immediately put to the test. The towns of Hanover, New Hampshire, and Norwich, Vermont, desired to operate a high school jointly. They obtained all necessary permissions from the appropriate federal and state agencies. When they were ready to issue bonds for the construction of facilities, bond counsel were unwilling to approve their validity. In *Dresden School District v. Norwich School District* (1964), the Vermont Supreme Court held that the bonds would be a valid obligation of the town of Norwich. The court reasoned that municipalities may be given power to deal with local matters. Education is a local matter, and traditionally local officials have been delegated the power to finance and administer local schools. Citing the recent amendment to the constitution, the court declared that the legislature had the authority to implement this local unit's ability to join with an interstate school district.

Following the *Dresden* case the court was faced with the issue of public funding of private educational institutions in *Vermont Educational Buildings Financing Agency v. Mann* (1968). There Bennington College and the College of St. Joseph the Provider (a religious institution) applied for funds for construction of educational facilities at their institutions from the plaintiff agency. On advice of counsel the chairman of the agency refused to execute leases and issue the necessary revenue bonds. Citing Section 68 of the constitution, the court held that the agency served a public purpose. As the general public benefit is the dominant interest, the act would be constitutional even though a private institution benefitted.

When a statute provides for an exemption from taxation, it must be strictly construed but not so as to defeat the purpose of the statute. The court in *Grand Lodge of Vermont F. & A. M. v. City of Burlington* (1932) held that this rule was not affected by this section of the constitution. In 1915 the court had held that an inheritance tax on a charitable bequest was in violation of the statute granting an exemption to a charitable "society or institution" (*In re Estate of Curtis*, 1915). In its discussion, the court agreed that exemption from taxation must be construed against those claiming benefits. The court declared the policy of the state to be favorable to religious or charitable institutions and thus held the exemption in this case valid.

However, this section does not grant a religious or charitable institution immunity from liability for injury caused by negligence (*Foster v. Roman Catholic Diocese of Vermont*, 1950).

SECTION 69. CHARTERS

> No charter of incorporation shall be granted, extended, changed or amended by special law, except for such municipal, charitable, educational, penal or reformatory corporations as are to be and remain under the patronage or control of the State; but the General Assembly shall provide by general laws for the organization of all corporations hereafter to be created. All general laws passed pursuant to this section may be altered from time to time or repealed.

This section was made part of the constitution when Article of Amendment 35 was adopted in 1913.

The University of Vermont and State Agricultural College sought to borrow money for dormitory construction. A federal lending agency questioned its authority to so borrow in light of a statute limiting the value of the property an educational institution could acquire or hold to $10 million. The university had substantially more property than that. The attorney general issued an opinion in which he decided that the university was an "instrument of the state" and therefore a public institution. He further declared that the statute applied to private educational corporations only and that the university need not be limited to property of the value of $10 million.

SECTION 70. WORKERS' COMPENSATION

> The General Assembly may pass laws compelling compensation for injuries received by employees in the course of their employment resulting in death or bodily hurt, for the benefit of such employees, their widows or next of kin. It may designate the class or classes of employers and employees to which such laws shall apply.

This workers' compensation provision was adopted by Article of Amendment 35 (1913). The legislature has implemented this section by enacting various acts set forth in chapter 9 of Title 21 of the Vermont Statutes Annotated. It has never been the subject of litigation.

SECTION 71. DECLARATION OF RIGHTS

The Declaration of the political rights and privileges of the inhabitants of this State, is hereby declared to be a part of the constitution of this commonwealth; and ought not to be violated, on any pretence whatsoever.

This section was lifted verbatim from Section 46 of the Pennsyvania Constitution of 1776 and was incorporated as Section 43 of the Vermont Constitution of 1777. It became Section 39 of the 1786 Constitution and Section 42 of the 1793 Constitution, and is the present Section 71. The section has never been subject to litigation.

SECTION 72. AMENDING THE CONSTITUTION

At the biennial session of the General Assembly of this State which convenes in A.D. 1975, and at the biennial session convening every fourth year thereafter, the Senate by a vote of two-thirds of its members, may propose amendments to this Constitution, with the concurrence of a majority of the members of the House of Representatives with the amendment as proposed by the Senate. A proposed amendment so adopted by the Senate and concurred in by the House of Representatives shall be referred to the next biennial session of the General Assembly; and if at that session a majority of the members of the Senate and a majority of the House of Representatives concur in the proposed amendment, it shall be the duty of the General Assembly to submit the proposal to a direct vote of the freemen of the state. Any proposed amendment submitted to a vote of the freemen of the state in accordance with this section which is approved by a majority of the freemen voting thereon shall become part of the Constitution of this State.

Prior to the submission of a proposed amendment to a vote of the freemen in accordance with this section, public notice of the proposed amendment shall be given by proclamation of the Governor.

The General Assembly shall provide for the manner of voting by the freemen on amendments proposed under this section, and shall enact legislation to carry the provisions of this section into effect.

Initially, the procedure for amending the constitution called for a Council of Censors to meet every seven years and recommend to a convention changes in the constitution. The constitutions of 1776 and 1793 continued this practice. It was not until 1870 that, through Article of Amendment 25, this procedure was superseded. In 1974, through Article of Amendment 45, the present procedure was adopted.

The question has arisen as to the alternate method of amending the constitution through a convention. The attorney general gave as his opinion that a convention could be called to amend the constitution (Opinion of the Attorney General, 1968). He reasoned that Article 7 of the Constitution permitted such amendment. He also determined that such procedure was not prohibited by this section.

A 1967 opinion of the attorney general stated that a limited constitutional convention could be convened by resolution of the House and Senate and ratified by a referendum (Opinion of the Attorney General, 1968). In the same opinion he determined that the only other method of revising the constitution was by following the provisions of this section. Thus he rejected the possibility of amendments effected by both houses with a referendum or a convention where the General Assembly constituted itself as the convention. "Provisions of a constitution regulating its own amendment, otherwise than by a convention, are not merely directory, but are mandatory" (Opinion of the Attorney General, 1968).

The House may not amend a proposal of amendment submitted by the Senate (Opinion of the Attorney General, 1972).

Having established a biennial term for the General Assembly, the question was asked whether proposals of amendment had to be acted upon during the biennium (Opinion of the Attorney General, 1972). The attorney general responded that the proposal must be acted upon before the session was ended *sine die*.

What would happen if the House concurred in the proposal of amendment one day and reconsidered its action the next day and refused to concur? The attorney general replied that the first vote was not necessarily determinative and that the last vote properly taken before the end of the biennium would be the final action by the House (Opinion of the Attorney General, 1972).

SECTION 73. APPORTIONMENT OF THE GENERAL ASSEMBLY

The General Assembly shall establish senatorial districts, within and including all of the state, and shall further establish representative districts within and including all of the state.

At the biennial session following the taking of each decennial census under the authority of Congress, and at such other times as the General Assembly finds necessary, it shall revise the boundaries of the legislative districts and shall make a new apportionment of its membership in order to maintain equality of representation among the respective districts as nearly as is practicable. The General Assembly may provide for establishment of a legislative apportionment board to advise and assist the General Assembly concerning legislative apportionment. If the General Assembly fails to revise the legislative districts as required in this section, the Supreme Court in appropriate legal proceedings brought for the purpose may order reapportionment of the districts.

This section was adopted initially by Article of Amendment 48 (1974). That amendment called for reapportionment after every second presidential election. The present language designating the decennial census was adopted by Article of Amendment 50 (1978). The section has not been litigated.

Temporary Provisions

SECTION 74. EXTENSION OF TERMS OF CERTAIN OFFICERS

The persons severally elected in 1912 to the offices mentioned in section 43 shall hold such offices until the term of their successors elected the first Tuesday next after the first Monday of November, A.D. 1914, shall begin as herein provided.

This section was adopted as Section 6 of Article of Amendment 30 (1913). It has not been litigated. It has expired by its own language.

SECTION 75. REVISION OF CHAPTER 2

The Justices of the Supreme Court are hereby authorized and directed to revise Chapter II of the Constitution by incorporating into said Chapter all amendments of the Constitution that are now or may be then in force and excluding there from all sections, clauses and words not in force and rearranging and renumbering the sections thereof under appropriate titles as in their judgment may be most logical and convenient; and said revised Chapter II as certified to the Secretary of State by said Justices or a majority thereof shall be a part of the Constitution of this State in substitution for existing Chapter II and all amendments thereof.

This section was adopted as Article of Amendment 36 (1913). It has not been litigated.

■ APPENDIX 1

Preamble to the Constitution of 1777

Whereas, all government ought to be instituted and supported for the security and protection of the community, as such, and to enable the individuals who compose it, to enjoy their natural rights, and the other blessings which the Author of existence has bestowed upon man; and whenever those great ends of government are not obtained, the people have a right, by common consent, to change it, and take such measures as to them may appear necessary to promote their safety and happiness.

And whereas, the inhabitants of this State have, (in consideration of protection only) heretofore acknowledged allegiance to the King of Great Britain, and the said King has not only withdrawn that protection, but commenced, and still continues to carry on, with unabated vengeance, a most cruel and unjust war against them; employing therein, not only the troops of Great Britain, but foreign mercenaries, savages and slaves, for the avowed purpose of reducing them to a total and abject submission to the despotic dominion of the British parliament, with many other acts of tyranny (more fully set forth in the declaration of Congress,) whereby all allegiance and fealty to the said King and his successors, are dissolved and at an end; and all power and authority derived from him, ceased in the American Colonies.

And whereas, the territory which now comprehends the State of *Vermont*, did antecedently, of right, belong to the government of *New Hampshire*; and the former Governor thereof, viz. his excellency *Benning Wentworth*, Esq., granted many charters of lands and corporations, within this State, to the present inhabitants and others. And whereas, the late Lieutenant Governor *Colden*, of *New York*, with others, did, in violation of the tenth command, covet those very lands; and by a false representation made to the court of Great Britain, (in the year 1764, that for the convenience of trade and administration of justice, the inhabitants were desirous of being annexed to that government,) obtained jurisdiction of those very identical lands, *ex-parte*; which ever was, and is disagreeable to the inhabitants. And whereas, the legislature of *New York*, ever have, and still continue to disown the good people of this State, in their landed property, which will appear in the complaints hereafter inserted, and in the 36th section of their present constitution, in which is established the grants of land made by that government.

They have refused to make re-grants of our lands to the original proprietors and occupants, unless at the exorbitant rate of 2300 dollars fees for each township; and did enhance the quitrent, three fold, and demanded an immediate delivery of the title derived before, from *New Hampshire*.

The judges of their supreme court have made a solemn declaration, that the charters, conveyances, etc., of the lands included in the before described premises, were utterly null and void, on which said title was founded; in consequence
of which declaration, writs of possession have been by them issued, and the sheriff of the county of Albany sent, at the head of six or seven hundred men, to enforce the execution thereof.

They have passed an act, annexing a penalty thereto, of thirty pounds fine and six months imprisonment, on any person who should refuse assisting the sheriff, after being requested, for the purpose of executing writs of possession.

The Governors, *Dúnmore, Tryon* and *Colden*, have made re-grants of several tracts of land, included in the premises, to certain favorite to certain favorite land
jobbers in the government of *New-York*, in direct violation of his Britannic majesty's express prohibition, in the year 1767.

They have issued proclamations, wherein they have offered large sums of money, for the purpose of apprehending those very persons who have dared boldly, and publicly, to appear in defence of their just rights.

They did pass twelve acts of outlawry, on the 9th day of March, A.D. 1774, impowering the respective judges of their supreme court, to award execution of death against those inhabitants in said district that they should judge to be offenders, without trial.

They have, and still continue, an unjust claim to those lands, which greatly retards emigration into, and the settlement of, this State.

They have hired foreign troops, emigrants from *Scotland*, at two different times, and armed them, to drive us out of possession.

They have sent the savages on our frontiers, to distress us.

They have proceeded to erect the counties of Cumberland and Glocester [sic],and establish courts of justice there, after they were discountenanced by the authority of Great Britain.

The free Convention of the State of *New-York*, at *Harlem*, in the year 1776, unanimously voted, "That all quit-rents formerly due to the King of Great Britain, are now due and owing to this Convention, or such future government as shall be hereafter established in this State."

In the several stages of the aforesaid oppressions, we have petitioned his Britannic majesty, in the most humble manner, for redress, and have, at very great expense, received several reports in our favor; and in other instances, wherein we have petitioned the late legislative authority of *New-York*, those petitions have been treated with neglect.

And whereas, the local situation of this State, from *New-York*, at the extream [sic] part, is upwards of four hundred and fifty miles from the seat of that government, which renders it extream [sic] difficult to continue under the jurisdiction of said State.

Therefore, it is absolutely necessary, for the welfare and safety of the inhabitants of this State, that it should be, henceforth, a free and independent State; and that a just, permanent and proper form of government, should exist in it, derived from, and founded on, the authority of the people only, agreeable to the direction of the honorable American Congress.

We the representatives of the freemen of *Vermont*, in General Convention met, for the express purpose of forming such a government, confessing the goodness of the Great Governor of the *Universe*, (who alone, knows to what degree of earthly happiness, mankind may attain, by perfecting the arts of government,) in permitting the people of this State, by common consent, and without violence, deliberately to form for themselves, such just rules as they shall think best for governing their future society; and being fully convinced that it is our indispensable duty, to establish such original principles of government, as will best promote the general happiness of the people of this State, and their posterity, and provide for future improvements, without partiality for, or prejudice against, any particular class, sect, or denomination of men whatever,—do, by virtue of authority vested in us, by our constituents, ordain, declare, and establish, the following declaration of rights, and frame of government, to be the CONSTITUTION of this COMMONWEALTH, and to remain in force therein, forever, unaltered, except in such articles, as shall, hereafter, on experience, be found to require improvement, and which shall, by the same authority of the people, fairly delegated, as this frame of government directs, be amended or improved, for the more effectual obtaining and securing the great end and design of all government, herein before mentioned.

■ APPENDIX 2

Articles of Amendment to the Constitution of 1793: 1828–1870

ARTICLE I (1828)

Article [1.] No person, who is not already a freeman of this state, shall be entitled to exercise the privileges of a freeman, unless he be a natural born citizen of this, or some one of the United States or until he shall have been naturalized agreeably to the acts of Congress.

ARTICLE II (1836)

Article [2.] The most numerous branch of the Legislature of this State shall hereafter be styled the House of Representatives.

ARTICLE III (1836)

Article [3.] The Supreme Legislative power of this State shall hereafter be exercised by a Senate and the House of Representatives; which shall be styled, "The General Assembly of the State of Vermont." Each shall have and exercise the like powers in all acts of Legislation; and no bill, resolution, or other thing which shall have been passed by the one, shall have the effect of, or be declared to be, a law, without the concurrence of the other. Provided, That all Revenue bills shall originate in the House of Representatives,—but the Senate may propose or concur with amendments, as on other bills. Neither House during the session of the General Assembly, shall, without the consent of the other, adjourn for more than three days, nor to any other place than that, in which the two Houses shall be sitting,—and in case of disagreement between the two Houses, with respect to adjournment, the governor may adjourn them to such time as he shall think proper.

ARTICLE IV (1836)

Article [**4.**] The Senate shall be composed of thirty Senators, to be of the freemen of the County for which they are elected, respectively, who are thirty years of age or upwards, and to be annually elected by the freemen of each County respectively.—Each County shall be entitled to one Senator, at least, and the remainder of the Senators shall be apportioned to the several Counties according to their population, as the same was ascertained by the last Census, taken under the authority of the United States,—regard being always had, in such apportionment, to the Counties having the greatest fraction.—But the several counties shall, until after the next Census of the United States, be entitled to elect, and have their Senators, in the following proportion, to wit:

Bennington County, two; Windham County, three; Rutland County, three; Windsor County, four; Addison County, three; Orange County, three; Washington County, two; Chittenden County, two; Caledonia County, two; Franklin County, three; Orleans County, one; Essex County, one; Grand Isle County, one.

The Legislature shall make a new apportionment of the Senators to the several Counties, after the taking of each Census of the United States, or Census taken, for the purpose of such apportionment, by order of the Government of this State—always regarding the above provisions of this article.

ARTICLE V (1836)

Article [**5.**] The freemen of the several towns in each County shall annually, give their votes for the Senators, apportioned to such County, at the same time, and under the same regulations, as are now provided for the election of Councillors.—And the person or persons equal in number to the number of Senators, apportioned to such County, having the greatest number of legal votes, in such County respectively, shall be the Senator or Senators of such County.—At every election of Senators, after the votes shall have been taken, the Constable or presiding officer, assisted by the Selectmen and civil authority present, shall sort and count the said votes, and make two lists of the names of each person, with the number of votes given for each annexed to his name, a record of which shall be made in the Town Clerk's office, and shall seal up said lists, separately, and write on each the name of the town, and these words, "Votes for Senator," or "Votes for Senators,"as the case may be, one of which lists shall be delivered, by the presiding officer, to the Representative of said town, (if any) and if none be chosen, to the Representative of an adjoining town, to be transmitted to the President of the Senate;—the other list, the said presiding officer, shall within ten days, deliver to the Clerk of the County Court, for the same County,—and the Clerk of each County Court, respectively, or in case of his absence, or disability, to the Sheriff of such County, or in case of the absence or disability, of both, to the High Bailiff of such County, on the tenth day after such election, shall publicly, open, sort, and count said votes;—and make a record of the same in the office of the Clerk of such County Court, a copy of which he shall transmit to the Senate:—and shall also within ten days thereafter, transmit to the person or persons elected, a certificate of his or their election. **Provided**, However, that the General Assembly shall have power to regulate by Law the mode of balloting for Senators, within the several Counties, and to prescribe the means, and the manner by which the result of the balloting shall be ascertained, and through which the Senators chosen shall be certified of their election, and for filling all vacancies in the Senate, which shall happen by death, resignation or otherwise. But they shall not have power to apportion the Senators to the several Counties, otherwise, than according to the population thereof agreeably to the provisions herein before ordained.

ARTICLE VI (1836)

Article [**6.**] The Senate shall have the like powers to decide on the election and qualifications of, and to expel any of its members, make its own rules, and appoint its own officers, as are incident to, or are possessed by, the House of Representatives. A majority shall constitute a quorum. The Lieut. Governor shall be President of the Senate, except when he shall exercise the force of Governor, or when his office shall be vacant, or in his absence, in which cases the Senate shall appoint one of its own members to be President of the Senate, pro tempore. And the President of the Senate shall have a casting vote, but no other.

ARTICLE VII (1836)

Article [7.] The Senate shall have the sole power of trying and deciding upon all impeachments—when sitting for that purpose, they shall be on oath, or affirmation, and no person shall be convicted, without the concurrence of two thirds of the members present. Judgment in cases of impeachment, shall not extend farther than to removal from office—and disqualification to hold or enjoy any office of honor, or profit, or trust, under this State. But the party convicted shall, nevertheless, be liable and subject to indictment, trial, judgment, and unishment, according to Law.

ARTICLE VIII (1836)

Article [**8.**] The Supreme Executive power of the State shall be exercised by the Governor, or, in case of his absence, or disability, by the Lieut. Governor; who shall have all the powers, and perform all the duties vested in, and enjoined upon the Governor and Council, by the Eleventh and Twenty-seventh Sections of the Second Chapter of the Constitution, as at present established, excepting that he shall not sit as a judge, in case of impeachment, nor grant reprieve or pardon in any such case; nor shall he command the forces of the State in person, in time of war, or insurrection; unless by the advice and consent of the Senate; and no longer than they shall approve thereof. The Governor may have a Secretary of civil and military affairs, to be by him appointed during pleasure, whose services he may at all times command; and for whose compensation provision shall be made by law.

ARTICLE IX (1836)

Article [**9.**] The votes for Governor, Lieut. Governor, and Treasurer, of the State, shall be sorted and counted, and the result declared, by a committee appointed by the Senate and House of Representatives. If, at any time, there shall be no election, by the freemen, of Governor, Lieut. Governor, and Treasurer, of the State, the Senate and House of Representatives shall, by a joint ballot, elect to fill the office, not filled by the freemen as aforesaid, one of the three candidates for such office, (if there be so many) for whom the greatest number of votes shall have been returned.

ARTICLE X (1836)

Article [**10.**] The Secretary of State, and all officers, whose elections are not otherwise provided for, and who under the existing provisions of the Constitution, are elected by the Council and House of Representatives, shall, hereafter, be elected by the Senate and House of Representatives, in joint assembly, at which the presiding officer of the Senate, shall preside; and such presiding officer in such joint assembly shall have a casting vote, and no other.

ARTICLE XI (1836)

Article [**11.**] Every bill which shall have passed the Senate and House of Representatives, shall, before it become a law, be presented to the Governor; if he approve, he shall sign it; if not, he shall return it, with his objections, in writing, to the House, in which it shall have originated; which shall proceed to reconsider it. If upon such reconsideration a majority of the House shall pass the bill, it shall, together with the objections, be sent to the other House, by which, it shall, likewise, be reconsidered, and if approved by a majority of that House, it shall become a law. But, in all such cases, the votes of both Houses shall be taken by yeas and nays, and the names of the persons, voting for or against the bill, shall be entered on the journal of each House, respectively. If any bill shall not be returned by the Governor, as aforesaid, within five days, (Sundays excepted) after it shall have been presented to him, the same shall become a law, in like manner, as if he had signed it; unless the two Houses, by their adjournment, within three days after the presentment of such bill, shall prevent its return; in which case, it shall not become a law.

ARTICLE XII (1836)

Article [**12.**] The Writ of Habeas Corpus shall in no case be suspended.—It shall be a writ, issuable of right; and the General Assembly shall make provision to render it a speedy and effectual remedy in all cases proper therefor.

ARTICLE XIII (1836)

Article [**13.**] Such parts and provisions only of the Constitution of this State, established by Convention on the ninth day of July, one thousand seven hundred and ninety-three, as are altered or superseded by any of the foregoing amendments, or are repugnant thereto, shall hereafter cease to have effect.

ARTICLES XIV, XV AND XVI (1850)

Article [**14.**] The Assistant Judges of the County Court shall be elected by the Freemen of their respective Counties.

Article [**15.**] Sheriffs and High Bailiffs shall be elected by the Freemen of their respective Counties.

Article [**16.**] State's Attorneys shall be elected by the Freemen of their respective Counties.

ARTICLE XVII (1850)

Article [**17.**] Judges of Probate shall be elected by the Freemen of their respective Probate Districts.

ARTICLE XVIII (1850)

Article [**18.**] Justices of the peace shall be elected by the Freemen of their respective towns; and towns having less than one thousand inhabitants may elect any number of Justices of the Peace not exceeding **five**; towns having one thousand, and less than two thousand inhabitants, may elect **seven**; towns having two thousand and less than three thousand inhabitants, may elect **ten**; towns having three thousand and less than five thousand inhabitants, may elect **twelve**; and towns having five thousand, or more inhabitants, may elect **fifteen** Justices of the Peace.

ARTICLE XIX (1850)

Article [**19.**] All the officers named in the preceding articles of amendment shall be annually elected by ballot and shall hold their offices for one year, said year commencing on the first day of December next after their election.

ARTICLE XX (1850)

Article [**20.**] The election of the several officers mentioned in the preceding articles, excepting town Representatives, shall be made at the times and in the manner now directed in the Constitution for the choice of Senators. And the presiding officer of each Freemen's meeting, after the votes shall have been taken, sorted and counted, shall, in open meeting, make a certificate of the names of each person voted for, with the number of votes given for each, annexed to his name and designating the office for which the votes were given, a record of which shall be made in the Town Clerk's office, and he shall seal up said certificate, and shall write thereon the name of the town and the words, **Certificate of Votes for… … … …** and add thereto, in writing, the title of the office voted for, as the case may be, and shall deliver such certificate to some Representative chosen as a member of the General Assembly, whose duty it shall be to cause such certificate of votes to be delivered to the Committee of the General Assembly appointed to canvass the same. And at the sitting of the General Assembly, next after such balloting for the officers aforesaid, there shall be a Committee appointed of and by the General Assembly, who shall be sworn to the faithful discharge of their duty and whose duty it shall be to examine such certificates and ascertain the number of votes given for each candidate, and the persons receiving the largest number of votes for the respective offices, shall be declared duly elected, and by such Committee be reported to the General Assembly and the officers so elected shall be commissioned by the Governor. And if two or more persons designated for any one of said offices, shall have received an equal number of votes, the General Assembly shall elect one of such persons to such office.

ARTICLE XXI (1850)

Article [**21.**] The term of office of the Governor, Lieutenant Governor, and Treasurer of the State, respectively, shall commence when they shall be chosen and qualified, and shall continue for the term of one year, or until their successors shall be chosen and qualified, or to the adjournment of the session of the Legislature, at which, by the constitution and laws, their successors are required to be chosen, and not after such adjournment. And the Legislature shall provide, by general law, declaring what officer shall act as Governor whenever there shall be a vacancy in both the offices of Governor and Lieutenant Governor, occasioned by a failure to elect, or by the removal from office, or by the death, resignation, or inability of both Governor and Lieutenant Governor, to exercise the powers and discharge the duties of the office of Governor; and such officer, so designated, shall exercise the powers and discharge the duties appertaining to the office of Governor accordingly until the disability shall be removed, or a Governor shall be elected. And in case there shall be a vacancy in the office of Treasurer, by reason of any of the causes enumerated, the Governor shall appoint a Treasurer for the time being, who shall act as Treasurer until the disability shall be removed, or a new election shall be made.

ARTICLE XXII (1850)

Article [**22.**] The Treasurer of the State shall, before entering upon the duties of his office, give sufficient security to the Secretary of State, in behalf of the State of Vermont, before the Governor of the State or one of the Judges of the Supreme Court. And Sheriffs and High Bailiffs, before entering upon the duties of their respective offices, shall give sufficient security to the Treasurer of their respective Counties, before one of the Judges of the Supreme Court, or the two Assistant Judges of the County Court of their respective Counties, in such manner and in such sums as shall be directed by the Legislature.

ARTICLE XXIII (1850)

Article [**23.**] The Senate shall be composed of thirty Senators, to be of the Freemen of the County for which they are elected, respectively, who shall have attained the age of thirty years, and they shall be elected annually by the Freemen of each County respectively.

The Senators shall be apportioned to the several Counties, according to the population, as ascertained by the census taken under the authority of Congress in the year 1840, regard being always had, in such apportionment to the Counties having the largest fraction, and giving to each County at least one Senator.

The Legislature shall make a new apportionment of the Senators to the several Counties, after the taking of each census of the United States, or after a census taken for the purpose of such apportionment, under the authority of this State, always regarding the above provisions of this article.

ARTICLE XXIV (1870)

Article [24.] Section 1. The General Assembly shall meet on the first Wednesday of October, biennially; the first election shall be on the first Tuesday of September, A.D. 1870; the first session of the General Assembly on the first Wednesday of October, A.D. 1870.

Section 2. The Governor, Lieutenant Governor, Treasurer of the State, senators, town representatives, assistant judges of the county court, sheriffs, high bailiffs, State's attorneys, judges of probate and justices of the peace, shall be elected biennially, on the first Tuesday of September, in the manner prescribed by the Constitution of the State.

Section 3. The term of office of the Governor, Lieutenant Governor and Treasurer of the State, respectively, shall commence when they shall be chosen and qualified, and shall continue for the term of two years, or until their successors shall be chosen and qualified, or to the adjournment of the session of the Legislature at which, by the Constitution and laws, their successors are required to be chosen, and not after such adjournment.

Section 4. The term of office of senators and town representatives shall be two years, commencing on the first Wednesday of October following their election.

Section 5. The term of office of the assistant judges of the county court, sheriffs, high bailiffs, State's attorneys, judges of probate and justices of the peace, shall be two years, and shall commence on the first day of December next after their election.

ARTICLE XXV (1870)

Article [25.] Section 1. At the session of the General Assembly of this State, A.D. 1880, and at the session thereof every tenth year thereafter, the Senate may, by a vote of two-thirds of its members, make proposals of amendment to the Constitution of the State, which proposals of amendment, if concurred in by a majority of the members of the House of Representatives, shall be entered on the journals of the two Houses, and referred to the General Assembly then next to be chosen, and be published in the principal newspapers of the State; and if a majority of the members of the Senate and of the House of Representatives of the next following General Assembly shall respectively concur in the same proposals of amendment, or any of them, it shall be the duty of the General Assembly to submit the proposals of amendment so concurred in to a direct vote of the freemen of the State; and such of said proposals of amendment as shall receive a majority of the votes of the freemen voting thereon shall become a part of the Constitution of this State.

Section 2. The General Assembly shall direct the manner of voting by the people upon the proposed amendments, and enact all such laws as shall be necessary to procure a free and fair vote upon each amendment proposed, and to carry into effect all the provisions of the preceding section.

Section 3. The House of Representatives shall have all the powers now possessed by the Council of Censors to order impeachments, which shall in all cases be by a vote of two-thirds of its members.

Section 4. The forty-third section of the second part of the Constitution of this State is hereby abrogated.

ARTICLE XXVI (1870)

Article [**26.**] The judges of the Supreme Court shall be elected biennially, and their term of office shall be two years.

ARTICLE XXVII (1883)

Article [**27.**] **Section 1.** The representatives having met on the day appointed by law for the commencement of a biennial session of the general assembly and chosen their speaker, and the senators having met, shall, before they proceed to business, take and subscribe the following oath in addition to the oath now prescribed,

"You ——— ——— do solemnly swear (or affirm) that you did not at the time of your election to this body, and that you do now hold, any office of profit or trust under the authority of Congress. So help you God. (Or in case of an affirmation) *under the pains and penalties of perjury."*

Section 2. The words "**office of profit or trust under the authority of Congress**" shall be construed to mean any office created directly or indirectly by Congress, and for which emolument is provided from the treasury of the United States.

ARTICLE XXVIII (1883)

Article [**28.**] **Section 1.** The Secretary of State and Auditor of Accounts shall be elected by the freemen of the State upon the same ticket with the Governor, Lieut. Governor and Treasurer.

Section 2. The Legislature shall carry this article into effect by appropriate legislation.

ARTICLE XXIX (1913)

Article [**29.**] Every bill which shall have passed the Senate and House of Representatives, shall, before it becomes law, be presented to the governor; if he approve, he shall sign it; if not, he shall return it, with his objections in writing, to the house, in which it shall have originated; which shall proceed to reconsider it. If upon such reconsideration, two-thirds of the members present of the house shall pass the bill, it shall, together with the objections, be sent to the other house, by which it shall, likewise, be reconsidered, and if approved by two-thirds of the members present of that house, it shall become a law.

But, in all such cases, the votes of both houses shall be taken by yeas and nays, and the names of the persons voting for or against the bill shall be entered on the journal of each house, respectively. If any bill shall not be returned by the governor, as aforesaid, within five days, (Sundays excepted) after it shall have been presented to him, the same shall become a law, in like manner, as if he had signed it; unless the two houses, by their adjournment within three days after the presentment of such bill, shall prevent its return; in which case, it shall not become a law.

ARTICLE XXX (1913)

Article [**30.**] **Section 1.** The general assembly shall meet biennially on the first Wednesday next after the first Monday of January, beginning in A.D. 1915.

Section 2. The governor, lieutenant-governor, treasurer, secretary of state, auditor of accounts, senators, town representatives, assistant judges of the county court, sheriffs, high bailiffs, state's attorneys; judges of probate and justices of the peace, shall be elected biennially, on the first Tuesday next after the first Monday of November, beginning in A.D. 1914.

Section 4. The term of office of senators and town representatives shall be two years, commencing on the first Wednesday next after the first Monday of January following their election.

Section 5. The term of office of the assistant judges of the county court, sheriffs, high bailiffs, state's attorneys, judges of probate and justices of the peace, shall be two years, and shall commence on the first day of February next after their election.

And that a new section, to be known as Section 6, be added as follows:

Section 6. The persons who shall be severally elected in 1912 to the offices mentioned in this article shall hold such offices until the term of their successors elected the first Tuesday next after the first Monday of November, A.D. 1914, shall begin as herein provided.

ARTICLE XXXI (1913)

Article [**31.**] The votes and proceedings of the General Assembly shall be printed (when one-third of the members of either house think is necessary), as soon as convenient after the end of the session, with the yeas and nays of the house of representatives on any question when required by five members, and of the senate when required by one senator (except where the votes shall be taken by ballot), in which case every member of either house shall have a right to insert the reasons of his vote upon the minutes.

ARTICLE XXXII (1913)

Article [**32.**] No person ought in any case, or in any time, to be declared guilty of treason or felony, by the legislature, nor to have his sentence upon conviction for felony commuted, remitted or mitigated by the legislature.

And that section 11 of Chapter 2 be amended by omitting the words "and murder" where they occur therein.

ARTICLE XXXIII (1913)

Article [**33.**]No charter of incorporation shall be granted, extended, changed or amended by special law, except for such municipal, charitable, educational, penal or reformatory corporations as are to be and remain under the patronage or control of the state; but the general assembly shall provide by general laws for the organization of all corporations hereafter to be created. All general laws passed pursuant to this article may be altered from time to time or repealed.

ARTICLE XXXIV (1913)

Article [**34.**] That wherever the words "judge" or "judges" are used in the Constitution of Vermont or amendments thereof, to designate a judge or judges of the supreme court, the words,"justice" or "justices" shall be substituted therefor, as the case may require.

ARTICLE XXXV (1913)

Article [**35.**] The general assembly may pass laws compelling compensation for injuries received by employees in the course of their employment resulting in death or bodily hurt, for the benefit of such employees, their widows or next of kin. It may designate the class or classes of employers and employees to which such laws shall apply.

ARTICLE XXXVI(1913)

Article [**36.**] That the judges of the supreme court be and are hereby authorized and directed to revise Chapter 2 of the constitution by incorporating into said chapter all amendments of the constitution that are now or may be then in force and excluding therefrom all sections, clauses and words not in force and rearranging and renumbering the sections thereof under appropriate titles as in their judgment may be most logical and convenient; and said revised Chapter 2 as certified to the secretary of state by said judges or a majority thereof shall be a part of the constitution of this state in substitution for existing Chapter 2 and all amendments thereof.

ARTICLE XXXVII (1924)

Article [**37.**] That all men are born equally free and independent, and have certain natural, inherent, and unalienable rights, amongst which are the enjoying and defending life and liberty, acquiring, possessing and protecting property, and pursuing and obtaining happiness and safety; therefore no person born in this country, or brought from over sea, ought to be holden by law, to serve any person as a servant, slave or apprentice, after he arrives to the age of twenty-one years, unless he is bound by his own consent, after he arrives to such age, or bound by law for the payment of debts, damages, fines, costs, or the like.

ARTICLE XXXVIII (1924)

Article [**38.**] That in all prosecutions for criminal offenses, a person hath a right to be heard by himself and his counsel; to demand the cause and nature of his accusation; to be confronted with the witnesses; to call for evidence in his favor, and a speedy public trial by an impartial jury of the country; without the unanimous consent of which jury, he cannot be found guilty; nor can he be compelled to give evidence against himself, nor can any person be justly deprived of his liberty, except by the laws of the land, or the judgment of his peers; provided, nevertheless, in criminal prosecutions for offenses not punishable by death or imprisonment in the state prison, the accused, with the consent of the prosecuting officer entered of record, may in open court or by a writing signed by him and filed with the court, waive his right to a jury trial and submit the issue of his guilt to the determination and judgment of the court without a jury.

ARTICLE XXXIX (1924)

Article [**39.**] In order that the freemen of the state may enjoy equally the benefit of election as equally as may be, each inhabited town in this state may, forever hereafter, hold elections therein and choose each one representative to represent them in the House of Representatives. Provided, however, that the General Assembly shall have the power to regulate by law the mode of filling all vacancies in the House of Representatives which shall happen by death, resignation or otherwise.

ARTICLE XL (1924)

Article [**40.**] Every person of the full age of twenty-one years, who is a natural born citizen of this or some one of the United States, or has been naturalized agreeably to the Acts of Congress, having resided in this state for the space of one whole year next before the election of representatives and who is of a quiet and peaceable behavior, and will take the following oath or affirmation, shall be entitled to all the privileges of a freeman of this state:

"You solemnly swear (or affirm) that whenever you give your vote or suffrage, touching any matter that concerns the State of Vermont, you will do it so as in your conscience you shall judge will most conduce to the best good of the same, as established by the Constitution, without fear or favor of any person."

ARTICLE XLI (1954)

Article [**41.**] Laws for the encouragement of virtue and prevention of vice and immorality, ought to be constantly kept in force, and duly executed; and a competent number of schools ought to be maintained in each town, or by towns jointly with the consent of the General Assembly, for the convenient instruction of youth. All religious societies, or bodies of men that may be united or incorporated for the advancement of religion and learning, or for other pious and charitable purposes, shall be encouraged and protected in the enjoyment of the privileges, immunities, and estates, which they injustice ought to enjoy, under such regulations as the General Assembly of this State shall direct.

ARTICLE XLII (1954)

Article [**42.**] The Representatives having met on the day appointed by law for the commencement of a biennial session of the General Assembly, and chosen their Speaker, and Senators having met, shall, before they proceed to business, take and subscribe the following oath, in addition to the oath prescribed in the foregoing section:

"You ——— ——— do solemnly swear (or affirm) that you did not at the time of your election to this body, and that you do not now, hold any office of profit or trust under the authority of Congress. So help you God. (Or in case of an affirmation) Under the pains and penalties of perjury."

The words "office of profit or trust under the authority of Congress" shall be construed to mean any office created directly or indirectly by Congress, and for which emolument is provided from the Treasury of the United States, other than that of a member of the commissioned or enlisted personnel in the reserve components of the armed forces of the United States while not on extended active duty.

No person in this State shall be capable of holding or exercising more than one of the following offices at the same time: Governor, Lieutenant-Governor, Justice of the Supreme Court, Treasurer of the State, member of the Senate, member of the House of Representatives, Surveyor-General, or Sheriff. Nor shall any person holding any office of profit or trust under the authority of Congress, other than a member of the commissioned or enlisted personnel in the reserve components of the armed forces of the United States while not on extended active duty, be eligible to any appointment in the Legislature, or to any executive or judiciary office under this State.

ARTICLE XLIII (1954)

Article [**43.**] The inhabitants of this State shall be trained and armed for its defense, under such regulations, restrictions, and exceptions, as Congress, agreeably to the Constitution of the United States, and the Legislature of this State, shall direct.

ARTICLE XLIV (1964)

Article [**44.**] Laws for the encouragement of virtue and prevention of vice and immorality ought to be constantly kept in force, and duly executed; and a competent number of schools ought to be maintained in each town unless the general assembly permits other provisions for the convenient instruction of youth. All religious societies, or bodies of men that may be united or incorporated for the advancement of religion and learning, or for other pious and charitable purposes, shall be encouraged and protected in the enjoyment of the privileges, immunities, and estates, which they in justice ought to enjoy, under such regulations as the general assembly of this state shall direct.

ARTICLE XLV (1974)

Article [**45.**] At the biennial session of the General Assembly of this State which convenes in A.D. 1975, and at the biennial session convening every fourth year thereafter, the Senate by a vote of two-thirds of its members, may propose amendments to this Constitution, with the concurrence of a majority of the members of the House of Representatives with the amendment as proposed by the Senate. A proposed amendment so adopted by the Senate and concurred in by the House of Representatives shall be referred to the next biennial session of the General Assembly; and if at that session a majority of the members of the Senate and a majority of the House of Representatives concur in the proposed amendment, it shall be the duty of the General Assembly to submit the proposal to a direct vote of the freemen of the state. Any proposed amendment submitted to a vote of the freemen of the state in accordance with this section which is approved by a majority of the freemen voting thereon shall become part of the Constitution of this State.

Prior to the submission of a proposed amendment to a vote of the freemen in accordance with this section, public notice of the proposed amendment shall be given by proclamation of the Governor.

The General Assembly shall provide for the manner of voting by the freemen on amendments proposed under this section, and shall enact legislation to carry the provisions of this section into effect.

ARTICLE XLVI (1974)

Article [46.] That in all prosecutions for criminal offenses, a person hath a right to be heard by himself and his counsel; to demand the cause and nature of his accusation; to be confronted with the witnesses; to call for evidence in his favor, and a speedy public trial by an impartial jury of the country; without the unanimous consent of which jury, he cannot be found guilty; nor can he be compelled to give evidence against himself; nor can any person be justly deprived of his liberty, except by the laws of the land, or the judgment of his peers; provided, nevertheless, in criminal prosecutions for offenses not punishable by death, the accused, with the consent of the prosecuting officer entered of record, may in open court or by a writing signed by him and filed with the court, waive his right to a jury trial and submit the issue of his guilt to the determination and judgment of the court without a jury.

Section 4. The judicial power of the State shall be vested in a unified judicial system which shall be composed of a Supreme Court, a Superior Court, and such other subordinate courts as the General Assembly may from time to time ordain and establish.

Section 25. The Treasurer of the State shall, before entering upon the duties of his office, give sufficient security to the Secretary of State, in behalf of the State of Vermont, before the Governor of the State or one of the Justices of the Supreme Court. And sheriffs, before entering upon the duties of their offices, shall give sufficient security in such manner and in such sums as shall be directed by the Legislature.

Section 28. The Courts of Justice shall be open for the trial of all causes proper for their cognizance; and justice shall be therein impartially administered, without corruption or unnecessary delay.

Section 30. Trials of issue, proper for the cognizance of a Jury as established by law or by judicial rules adopted by the Supreme Court not inconsistent with law, in the Supreme Court, the Superior Court and other subordinate courts, shall be by Jury, except where parties otherwise agree; and great care ought to be taken to prevent corruption of partiality in the choice and return, or appointment of Juries.

Section 45. The Assistant Judges shall be elected by the freemen of their respective districts as established by law. Their term of office shall be four years and shall commence on the first day of February next after their election.

Sheriffs shall be elected by the freemen of their respective districts as established by law. Their term of office shall be four years and shall commence on the first day of February next after their election.

State's Attorneys shall be elected by the freemen of their respective districts as established by law. Their term of office shall be four years and shall commence on the first day of February next after their election.

Section 46. Judges of Probate shall be elected by the freemen of their respective districts as established by law. The General Assembly may establish by law qualifications for the election to and holding of such office. Their term of office shall be four years and shall commence on the first day of February next after their election.

Section 47. Justices of the Peace shall be elected by the freemen of their respective towns; and towns having less than one thousand inhabitants may elect any number of Justices of the Peace not exceeding five; towns having one thousand and less than two thousand inhabitants, may elect seven; towns having two thousand and less than three thousand inhabitants, may elect ten; towns having three thousand and less than five thousand inhabitants, may elect twelve; and towns having five thousand, or more inhabitants, may elect fifteen Justices of the Peace. Justices of the Peace shall not exercise judicial powers, except that they may serve as magistrates when so commissioned by the Supreme Court.

Section 49. The manner and certification of election and filling of vacancies in the offices of Assistant Judges, Sheriffs, State's Attorneys, Judges of Probate and Justices of the Peace shall be as established by law.

Section 28a. The Supreme Court shall consist of the Chief Justice of the State and four associate justices of the Supreme Court.

Section 28b. (1). The Supreme Court shall exercise appellate jurisdiction in all cases, criminal and civil, under such terms and conditions as it shall specify in rules not inconsistent with law. The Supreme Court shall have original jurisdiction only as provided by law, but it shall have the power to issue all writs necessary or appropriate in aid of its appellate jurisdiction. The Supreme Court shall have administrative control of all the courts of the state, and disciplinary authority concerning all judicial officers and attorneys at law in the State.

Section 28b. (2). All other courts of this State shall have original and appellate jurisdiction as provided by law. All courts except the Supreme Court may be divided into geographical and functional divisions as provided by law or by judicial rules adopted by the Supreme Court not inconsistent with law. The jurisdiction of geographical and functional divisions shall be as provided by law or by judicial rules not inconsistent with law. The courts of this state may exercise equity jurisdiction as well as law jurisdiction in civil proceedings as may be provided by law or by judicial rules not inconsistent with law.

Section 28c. (1). The Governor, with the advice and consent of the Senate, shall fill a vacancy in the office of Chief Justice of the State, associate Justice of the Supreme Court or judge of any other court, except the office of Assistant Judge and of Judge of Probate, from a list of nominees presented to him by a judicial nominating body established by the General Assembly having authority to apply reasonable standards of selection.

Section 28c. (2). When the Senate is not in session, the Governor may make an interim appointment to fill a vacancy in the office of chief justice, associate justice of the Supreme Court or judge of any other court, except the office of Assistant Judge and of Judge of Probate, from a list of nominees presented by the judicial nominating body. A justice or judge so appointed shall hold office, with all the powers incident to the office, until the Senate convenes and acts upon the appointment submitted by the Governor. Thereafter, the appointee shall continue in office if the Senate consents to the appointment. If the appointment is not confirmed upon vote of the Senate, the appointment shall be terminated and a vacancy in the office will be created.

Section 28c. (3). The justices of the Supreme Court and judges of all subordinate courts, except Assistant Judges and Judges of Probate, shall hold office for terms of six years except when holding office under an interim appointment. At the end of the initial six year term and at the end of each six year term thereafter, such justice or judge may give notice in the manner provided by law of his desire to continue in office. When such justice or judge gives the required notice, the question of his continuance in office shall be submitted to the General Assembly and he shall continue in office for another term of six years unless a majority of the members of the General Assembly voting on the question vote against his continuing in office.

Section 28c. (4). All justices of the Supreme Court and judges of all subordinate courts shall be retired at the end of the calendar year in which they attain seventy years of age or at the end of the term of election during which they attain seventy years of age, as the case may be, and shall be pensioned as provided by law. The chief justice may from time to time appoint retired justices and judges to special assignments as permitted under the rules of the Supreme Court.

Section 28c. (5). The justices of the Supreme Court and judges of all subordinate courts shall hold office during good behavior for the terms for which they are appointed. The Supreme Court in the exercise of its disciplinary power over the judiciary of the state may suspend justices of the Supreme Court and judges of all subordinate courts from the judicial function for such cause and in such manner as may be provided by law.

The General Assembly may establish procedures for the implementation of the provisions of this section.

Section 28d. The Supreme Court shall make and promulgate rules governing the administration of all courts, and shall make and promulgate rules governing practice and procedure in civil and criminal cases in all courts. Any rule adopted by the Supreme Court may be revised by the General Assembly.

ARTICLE XLVII (1974)

Article [**47.**] Every person of the full age of eighteen years who is a citizen of the United States, having resided in this State for the period established by the General Assembly and who is of a quiet and peaceable behavior, and will take the following oath or affirmation, shall be entitled to all the privileges of a freeman of this state:

You solemnly swear (or affirm) that whenever you give your vote or suffrage, touching any matter that concerns the State of Vermont, you will do it so as in your conscience you shall judge will most conduce to the best good of the same, as established by the Constitution, without fear or favor of any person.

ARTICLE XLVIII (1974)

Article [**48.**] The House of Representatives shall be composed of one hundred fifty Representatives. The freemen of each representative district established by law shall elect one or two Representatives from that district, the number from each district to be established by the General Assembly.

In establishing representative districts, which shall afford equality of representation, the General Assembly shall seek to maintain geographical compactness and contiguity and to adhere to boundaries of counties and other existing political subdivisions.

Section 15. No person shall be elected a Representative or a Senator until he has resided in this State two years, the last year of which shall be in the legislative district for which he is elected.

Section 18. The Senate shall be composed of thirty Senators to be of the freemen of the senatorial district from which they are elected. The freemen of each senatorial district established by law shall elect one or more Senators from that district, the number from each district to be established by the General Assembly.

In establishing senatorial districts, which shall afford equality of representation, the General Assembly shall seek to maintain geographical compactness and contiguity and to adhere to boundaries of counties and other existing political subdivisions.

Section 36. Senators and Representatives shall be elected to office at a general election to be held biennially on the first Tuesday next after the first Monday of November, A.D. 1974.

Section 37. The manner of election, certification, and filling of vacancies in office of Senators and Representatives shall be as established by law.

Section 38. The term of office of Senators and Representatives shall be two years, commencing on the first Wednesday next after the first Monday of January following their election.

Section 72. The General Assembly shall establish senatorial districts, within and including all of the state, and shall further establish representative districts within and including all of the state.

At the biennial session following each second presidential election, and at such other times as the General Assembly finds necessary, it shall revise the boundaries of the legislative districts and shall make a new apportionment of its membership in order to maintain equality of representation among the respective districts as nearly as it is practicable. The General Assembly may provide for establishment of a legislative apportionment board to advise and assist the General Assembly concerning legislative apportionment. If the General Assembly fails to revise the legislative districts as required in this section, the Supreme Court in appropriate legal proceedings brought for that purpose may order reapportionment of the districts.

ARTICLE 49 (1982)

Article [**49.**] Excessive bail shall not be exacted for bailable offenses. All persons, unless sentenced, or unless committed for offenses punishable by death or life imprisonment when the evidence of guilt is great, shall be bailable by sufficient sureties. Persons committed for offenses punishable by death or life imprisonment, when the evidence of guilt is great, shall not be bailable as a matter of right. No person shall be imprisoned for debt.

ARTICLE 50 (1986)

Article [**50.**] The General Assembly shall establish senatorial districts within and including all of the state, and shall further establish representative districts within and including all of the state.

At the biennial session following the taking of each decennial census under the authority of Congress, and at such other times as the General Assembly finds necessary, it shall revise the boundaries of the legislative districts and shall make a new apportionment of its membership in order to maintain equality of representation among the respective districts as nearly as is practicable. The General Assembly may provide for establishment of a legislative apportionment board to advise and assist the General Assembly concerning legislative apportionment. If the General Assembly fails to revise the legislative apportionment districts as required in this section, the Supreme Court in appropriate legal proceedings brought for the purpose may order reapportionment of the districts.

■ BIBLIOGRAPHICAL ESSAY

Much has been written about the formation of the state of Vermont. The documents of the various conventions have been collected in *Vermont State Papers,* compiled and edited by William Slade, Jr., Secretary of State (Middlebury: J. W. Copeland, Printer, 1823).

More readable histories of the formation are contained in an article by Gary Aichele, "Making the Vermont Constitution 1777–1824," in 56 *Vermont History* 166 (Summer 1988); a book by Matt Bushnell Jones, *Vermont in the Making,* 1750–1777 (1939. Reprint. New York: AMS Books, 1968); and *Constitutional History of Vermont* by John W. Rowell, contained in volume 3 of *The New England States* (Boston: D. H. Hurd, 1897).

Two early histories give a more detailed story of the formative years of the state of Vermont. They are Benjamin H. Hall's *History of Eastern Vermont* (New York: D. Appleton, 1858) and Hiland Hall's *The History of Vermont from Its discovery to Its Admission into the Union in 1791* (Albany: J. Munsell, 1868). Charles T. Morrissey's *Vermont: A History* (New York: Norton, 1981) brings Vermont history up to 1981. (*The Natural and Political History of the State of Vermont* by Ira Allen (1798. Reprint. London: Charles E. Tuttle, 1969) is the only book written by a major figure in the formation of the state. Some inaccuracies have been corrected in the reprint edition.

The Vermont Constitution of 1777 was modeled on the Pennsylvania Constitution of 1776. John N. Schaeffer wrote *A Comparison of the First Constitutions of Vermont and Pennsylvania,* which appears in 43 *Vermont History* 33 (Winter 1975). It detailed 27 substantive changes from Pennsylvania and shows the conservatism of the Vermont Constitution of 1777. John H. Watson, as chief justice of the state, addressed the Vermont Bar Association in 1921. His speech, "In re Vermont Constitution of 1777, as Regards Its Adoption," in *Vermont Historical Society Proceedings 1920–1921* has a good discussion of Article 1 and slavery. Watson also argued that the Constitution of 1777 was adopted at Windsor and needed no ratification.

Little has been written about the subsequent development of the constitution. We are, however, indebted to Paul S. Gillies and D. Gregory Sanford for compiling *The Records of the Council of Censors* (Essex, Vt: Offset House, 1991), which contains the text of the three original constitutions (1777, 1786, 1793) as well as the journals of each Council of Censors, from 1785 to 1869 including their resolutions and addresses and the results of their recommendations. It is an essential reference for anyone researching the development of the constitution through the years of the council.

In Daniel Chipman's *A Memoir of Thomas Chittenden* (Middlebury, Vt.: Chipman, 1849) he argues for the dissolution of the council.

The reports of the conventions called by the Council of Censors to amend the constitution can be found in the state archivist's office in Montpelier, Vermont. They are not, to my knowledge, compiled in one book. The journal of the Vermont Constitutional Convention of 1793 may be found in *Proceedings of the Vermont Historical Society* (1921), 185.

"Origins of the ten-year time-lock in the Vermont Constitution" is the subject and also the title of an article by John Williams and Kay Breer appearing in 37 *Vermont History* (1969), 133. Frank M. Bryan's 'Reducing the Time-Lock in the Vermont Constitution: An Analysis of the 1974 Referendum," in 44 *Vermont History* (Winter 1976), is an interesting article on the history of the time lock in amending the Vermont Constitution.

There are various reports of committees appointed by various legislatures to report back possible amendments. Articles will also be found in volumes of the *Vermont Law Review*, published by the Vermont Law School.

The following articles on Vermont history, arranged chronologically, may also be of interest:

Sidney G. Morse. "The Representation Issue in Vermont a Century Ago." 21 *Vermont Quarterly* 83 (April 1953):85.

Harris E. Thurber. "The Vermont Judicial System: Some Characteristics." 23 *Vermont History* 177 (July 1955).

Harris E. Thurber. "Some Values of the Vermont Community, Part I." 25 *Vermont History*194 (July 1957); *Part II. 25 Vermont History* 292 (October 1957).

Clyde Fussell. "The Emergence of Public Education as a Function of the State of Vermont." 28 *Vermont History* 179 (July 1960). See section on education and the state constitution at p. 187.

Nathaniel Hendricks. "A New Look at the Ratification of the Vermont Constitution of 1777." 34 *Vermont History* 136–140 (1966).

Robert V. Daniels and Robert H. Daniels. "The Vermont Constitutional Referendum of 1969: An Analysis." 38 *Vermont History* 152–156 (Spring 1970).

William C. Hill. "Vermont's Judicial Crisis of 1914–1915." 38 *Vermont History* 124–138

"Collections of the Vermont Historical Society." Montpelier, (1870) Vol. 1, pp. 331–486.

Ira Allen's *The Natural and Political History of Vermont*, Vol. 1. This volume and Volume 2 duplicate much of Slade's papers but do contain the original Ira Allen history.

Finally, Murray Bookchin wrote a small booklet, *The Vermont Constitution: A Legacy Worth Saving* (Burlington: Green Program Project, 1987), which is worth reading.

TABLE OF CASES

A

B

C

D

E

F

G

H

I

J

K

L

M

Montpelier, Demers v., 120 VT. 380, 141 A.2d 676 (1958), **39, 40**
Montpelier National Bank, Vermont Home Mortgage Credit Agency v., 128 VT. 272, 262 A.2d 445 (1970), **61, 110**
Montpelier v. East Montpelier, 29 VT. 12 (1856), **114**
Morse, State v., 126 VT. 314, 229 A.2d 232 (1967), **71**
Morse v. Ward, 102 VT. 433, 150 A. 132 (1930), **132**
Moses, In re, 122 VT. 36, 163 A.2d 868 (1960), **68**
Municipal Charters, In re, 86 VT. 562, 86 A.307 (1913), **114**
Murphy, State v., 134 VT. 106, 353 A.2d 346 (1976), **67**
Muzzy v. Curtis, 127 VT. 516, 253 A.2d 149 (1969), **138**

N

National Land and Loan Co. v. Mead, 60 VT. 257, 14 A.689 (1888), **116**
New England Trout & Salmon Club v. Mather, 68 VT. 338, 35 A.323 (1895), **166**
Nichols, Taylor v., 29 VT. 104 (1856), **128**
Niles, State v., 78 VT. 266, 62 A.795 (1906), **166**
North Troy, Hoyt v., 93 VT. 8, 105 A.33 (1918), **39**
Norton, State v., 45 VT. 258 (1872), **165**
Nonvich School District, Dresden School District v., 124 VT. 227,203 A.2d 598 (1964), **168**

O

Oakes, State v., #89-506 (VT.) (1990), **86**
Oliver v. United States, 466 U.S. 170 (1984), **32, 85**
Ovitt, State v., 126 VT. 320, 229 A.2d 237 (1967), **75**

P

Pabst v. Commissioner of Taxes, 136 VT. 126, 388 A.2d 1181 (1978), **60**
Park, Town of Bennington v., 50 VT. 178 (1877), **114**
Parker, Sowrna v., 112 VT. 241, 22 A.2d 513 (1941), **39, 47**
Peck v. Douglas, 148 VT. 128 530 A.2d 551 (1987), **135**
Pennsylvania, Bell's Gap Railroad v., 134 U.S. 232 (1890), **61**
Perkins, Hazen v., 92 VT. 414, 105 A.249 (1918), **167**
Perrault, Choquette v., 153 VT. 45, 569 A.2d 455 (1989), **55**
Perry, Smith v., 26 VT. 279 (1854), **163**
Persons, State v., 114 VT. 435, 46 A.2d 854 (1946), **71**
Peterson, State v., 41 VT. 504 (1869), **66, 75, 138**
Petition of Dusablon, 126 VT. 362, 230 A.2d 797 (1967), **156**
Petitions of Davenport et al., In re, 129 VT. 546, 283 A.2d 452 (1971), **105**
Pforzheirner, United States v., 826 F.2d 200 (2nd Cir.) (1987), **85**
Picknell, State v., 142 VT. 215, 454 A.2d 711 (1982), **80**
Pierce, State v., 120 VT. 373, 141 A.2d 419 (1958), **79**
Plirnpton v. Somerset, 33 VT. 283 (1860), **88, 138**
Potter, State v., 148 VT. 53, 529 A.2d 163 (1987), **73, 85**
Poulin v. Danville, 128 VT. 161, 260 A.2d 208 (1969), **62**
Powers, Courser v., 34 VT. 517 (1861), **156**
Powers, In re, 25 VT. 261 (1853), **66**
Pray, State v., 133 VT. 537, 346 A.2d 227 (1975), **140, 136**

Q

R

S

T

U

V

W

Y

Z

INDEX

About the Author

WILLIAM C. HILL is a retired justice of the Vermont Supreme Court.

www.ingramcontent.com/pod-product-compliance
Ingram Content Group UK Ltd.
Pitfield, Milton Keynes, MK11 3LW, UK
UKHW021134160926
475595UK00020B/40

9 780199 779024